SOUTH SIDE Boy

Roger Wiltz

authorHOUSE®

AuthorHouse™
1663 Liberty Drive
Bloomington, IN 47403
www.authorhouse.com
Phone: 1 (800) 839-8640

Published by AuthorHouse 02/15/2019

ISBN: 978-1-5462-7769-9 (sc)
ISBN: 978-1-5462-7767-5 (hc)
ISBN: 978-1-5462-7768-2 (e)

Library of Congress Control Number: 2019900932

Cover design by Lisa Leis of Creative Signworks

Print information available on the last page.

This book is printed on acid-free paper.

Dedication

To my father, John L. Wiltz. Whatever admirable traits I may possess can probably be traced back to him. Thanks Dad!

Table Of Contents

Foreword..ix

Book I – The South Side of Chicago

My Chicago 1
Good Times...21
School Days 28
Hobbies and Pass-times.. 44
Perverts and Predators 49
A Time of Racial Conflict..52
The Threat of Nuclear Annihilation 57
Summer Employment 59
A Skeleton in our Closet..69

Book II South Dakota

The College Years 1960-1964..73
Fall 1964..94
Willow Lake, SD...96
The Accident 100
The Parkston, SD Years - 1966-1971...103
The Burke, SD Years – 1971-1976...107

Book III – The Wagner Years 1976 – Present

A Brief Job Description and My First Year.................................... 115

Parents and Discipline... 117

The Fire.. 120

B&R Enterprises 121

Wagner High School's Finest Hour 123

The Wiltz Girls..125

My Brother's Suicide 128

Jury Duty..130

The School Bus Incident...133

Life Isn't Fair..136

The Yankton Sioux Tribe..139

Tripp-Delmont School – Golden Years in Education...................147

Rotary.. 150

Epilogue.. 151

Foreword

Though no particular accomplishments in my life warrant an autobiography, I feel like the man on the television insurance commercial when he says, "We know a thing or two because we've seen a thing or two."

I don't know that everything I relate is 100% accurate, but I have made every effort to tell the truth. The accounts and descriptions I give you are how I perceived them, and my memory may have faded over the many years in some instances.

While I have made an effort to adhere to chronological order, I believe that a strict order of events might become confusing. Subject by subject, rather than year by year, seemed more orderly. I also developed the subject matter by focusing on what I consider to be defining moments in my life.

As a lifetime educator in public schools, I believe my career spanned a transition from discipline in the home and discipline in our schools to the problems we have in today's public schools. Missing are student consequences and accountability. All but gone are the parents who once bragged to me, "When I got in trouble at school, I was in twice as much trouble at home!"

Other than today's lack of respect for teachers, parents/guardians, and authority in general, the academic bar has fallen. ACT/SAT entrance exams have been watered down. Ability to write has fallen by the wayside. Generations have passed since mastery of basic skills was a graduation requirement.

I don't know that I can accurately give the causes for this tragic decline, but I do know of some trends that seem to parallel our current state of affairs. Of course, what I say of family life isn't true of all families today.

The rise of illicit drug use is part of the equation. When I graduated from college in 1964, one didn't smell marijuana in dormitory halls, but I'm told it followed soon afterward.

When I was an impressionable child during the fifties, moms were full-time housewives who were at home when kids came home from school. This spelled "supervision." Ever so gradually the outside-the-home working mom evolved, a trend whose infancy was probably spawned in war plants during WWII. In the sixties I can recall the wives of friends paying babysitters as much as they made at their workplaces. They felt like they had to get away. What, if anything, was gained?

I believe that moms went to work for want of material goods. In 1950 Chicago, not every family had a vehicle. Today three might be the norm. If a home had a garage, it was a single car unit. The same was true of attached garages. Today we have a three-car garage. Most homes didn't have a television set. Now TV sets are often found in children's bedrooms. A single bath home was the norm. Two bath homes are now a necessity even though family size has diminished.

At some point in transition, discipline became child abuse. Up in our attic on Sangamon Street, I had my bare butt whipped with dad's leather belt on more than one occasion. I had it coming, and I needed it. Remember the 1983 movie "A Christmas Story"? Nine-year-old Ralphie uttered the F-word while helping his dad change a tire. The exact same thing happened in our home when I was that age, and I sat on a stool in the middle of the kitchen with an orange bar of Lifebuoy soap in my mouth for what seemed like hours. It worked. I never use the word, and I never heard my parents use it.

The family unit with a mom and dad as biological parents has self-destructed. Divorce has become too easy, and the courage to work through hard times is a thing of the past. Single-parent families have become somewhat of a norm. Somewhere in this scenario churches have fallen by the wayside.

With a lifetime career in education, I feel I have gained expertise in the field. I know that I have touched on some highly effective classroom techniques that I want to share with fellow educators, and I believe my thoughts are well worth reading for all classroom teachers as well as administrators.

One needs to keep in mind that I'm writing about the times. Martin Luther King wasn't a hero in 1960, and athletes weren't paid many millions of dollars to swing a ball bat, shoot baskets, or score touchdowns.

To this day I could not tell you whether my parents were Democrats or Republicans. I do know that they voted for the person and didn't adhere to party lines. In searching my memory for clues, I recall that my father didn't like Roosevelt and often inferred that FDR coerced the Japanese into attacking Pearl Harbor. I remember both Mom and Dad being very supportive of both Truman, a Democrat, and Eisenhower, a Republican.

Book I — The South Side of Chicago

My Chicago

For the most part, Chicago is laid out in a grid of perfect square miles with eight blocks to a mile. Generally, north-south streets have names while east-west streets are numbered. The numbered east-west streets have a major through street with stop lights every mile while the named north-south streets are of the same design. An occasional diagonal such as Vincennes Avenue, an old Indian trail that ran just west of our home, passed through the grid and paralleled for a stretch The Rock Island Line's commuter trains to the downtown LaSalle Street Station.

The intersection of State and Madison Streets is the heart of the grid with Madison separating the North and South sides. On my home South Side, 63rd, 71st, 79th, 87th, 95th, 103rd, and 111th Streets are major arteries. Going west from State Street, Halsted Street is 800 West or eight blocks. Ashland Avenue is 1600 West, followed every mile by Western Avenue, Kedzie, Pulaski, etc.

Chicago wasn't one big homogenous metropolis. It was a *potpourri* of over 200 interconnected and diverse communities each with its own neighborhood pride. Culture was often a part of the mix. When I met someone who said they were from Chicago, I asked them where they were from. They knew exactly what I meant. I was from Longwood. I went to high school in Roseland. Beverly lay to the west, Brainerd to the northwest, and Gresham to the north. Hegewisch bordered Indiana on the southeast. Morgan Park was south.

It is a personal perception that the South Side was a blue collar "roll

1

your sleeves up" population of factory people while the North Side was a white collar collection of wealthier neighborhoods. Such was my view of Lincoln Park, Evanston, Winnetka, etc. Depending upon which way the wind was blowing in our neighborhood, we could smell Nabisco graham crackers to the northwest, General Mills Cheerios from the east, and Sherwin-Williams paint from the southeast.

Until my job as a truck driver for Galassi Cut Stone during the summer of 1961, the North Side and the Western suburbs were as foreign to me as Eastern Europe. Along with the truck deliveries, dating brought me to North Side institutions including Riverview at Western & Belmont, Wrigley Field at Clark & Addison, and Ravinia Park in Highland Park.

My maternal grandmother had a summer cottage at Cedar Lake, Indiana that consumed much of my summer times. Once I had a driver's license, I became familiar with the Southeast and the route to the lake. The summers of 1963 and 1964 were spent working for Republic Steel, a job that familiarized me with East Chicago.

As a child, I grew up on the corner at 9601 S. Sangamon Street knowing that I wasn't to cross 95th Street to the north and Halsted Street to the east. Oakdale Park, which lay from 95th Street to 96th Street north and south, and from Morgan Street to Genoa Street east and west, became my after school stomping grounds.

My best childhood friend, David Trisko, was a key figure in my childhood. We were the same age and same grade, and we both attended St. Margaret's grammar school. David lived at 9544 S. Peoria Street, and it was necessary for him to pass our house on his way to school. This is no doubt how we met. Having younger brothers the same age, my brother, John, and his brother, Robert or Bobby, added similarities to our backgrounds.

David and I spent a lot of time together until different high schools more or less parted our ways. Dave went to the new Brother Rice High School on a 100th and Pulaski while I went to Mendel. At about this same time, the Trisko family moved to Oak Lawn, a western suburb, while we remained in the old neighborhood.

David's father, Clarence "Bud" Trisko, rose to the top of IBM's corporate ladder. At our 50th year St. Margaret's reunion, I asked Dave if he knew to what his father attributed his success. Dave said that they had once talked about it, and that his father said there were two things. Hire people who are smarter than you are, and fire those who aren't getting the job done. Over the years, I've seen these as profound bits of wisdom.

If I were to talk about the differences between now and then, I would certainly mention people's willingness to walk. Kids walked to school, and two miles wasn't too far. We often walked to school and back twice a day! Dads walked to and from train stations and bus stops. Moms, dads, and kids walked to grocery stores with two-wheel carts. Not everyone had a car. Grandma Olson, my mother's mother, lived at 8024 S. Aberdeen Street. My mother would frequently put my brother and me in a buggy and walk us the three miles (one way) to grandma's and back.

A second major difference related to family structure. The television shows "Father Knows Best" and "Leave It to Beaver" were doses of reality. The mothers of all my friends were full-time mothers and housewives. Dads walked in the back door at 6:00 p.m. after a day's work. If there was such a thing as divorce, I never saw it. Broken or single-parent homes were non-existent in my wonderful little world.

A third point that comes to mind is paying for an education. In 1960, a good summer job and a part-time on campus job would pay for a college education. School loans weren't necessary. Since that time, the cost of a college education has surged well ahead of one's ability to earn enough money during the summer.

Granted, my summer jobs paid well. However, it was a time when students went to the job. One of my best friends at Republic Steel came from Winnipeg, Manitoba and stayed with an aunt over the summer. Our daughters went to the job in the '80's. One lived in Sioux Falls with her grandmother, and another took a nanny job in Connecticut.

One of my very earliest recollections was that of the adults gathered around our radio, a big floor model in a cabinet. This seemed to occur in the early evening, and the news was often war related. I can also remember radio programs such as "The Lone Ranger" and "The Green Hornet" although they were not as important to me as early television.

The advent of television was monumental. In 1948 we had the first television set on the block, an Admiral console with a 10" screen. On Saturday afternoons neighbors came over to watch White Sox and Cubs games on WGN-TV with Jack Brickhouse doing the play by play.

The early television I remember included Kukla, Fran, and Ollie, a Burr Tillstrom creation with Fran Allison talking with puppets Kukla and Ollie the dragon. Our favorite program was Howdy Doody, a marionette puppet, with Buffalo Bob and Clarabelle the clown. I also watched Uncle Mistletoe. Mom and dad wouldn't miss the Ed Sullivan Show on Sunday night, and mom was devoted to Arthur Godfrey. My mother's Uncle Walter Olson brought mom a portable TV with a 7" screen that sat on the kitchen counter so she could watch Arthur Godfrey. I know mom bought Pillsbury products because of Godfrey.

Early television also carried serials on kid's shows such as Flash Gordon, Ace Drummond, and Clyde Beatty. I best remember Flash played by Buster Crabbe. Flash and his partners, Dale Arden and Dr. Zarkov, were in constant conflict with Ming the Merciless on the planet Mongo. I'm guessing these old serials once played in movie houses during the 1930's.

I believe it was in the middle 50's that Art Linkletter hosted the

4

Sunday afternoon TV show "People Are Funny." The program became especially interesting when a next door neighbor became part of the act. Bill and Della Smith lived next door to us on Sangamon Street. They had two daughters, Ann and Barbara, who were older than me. Barb became a weekly show guest when a computer matched her to some guy according to mutual interests, values, etc. They reported that their romance was becoming serious, but her mother confided in us that there was nothing to it.

Other than the Smiths next door, one other neighbor on our block comes to mind, and that was the Benelli family. As I ran down the alley behind our houses one day, I discovered the severed head of a horse stuck over the top of their backyard picket fence. I had no idea then of the significance, but after seeing *The Godfather* movie, I have to believe the incident had mafia connotations.

I don't recall exactly when, but I do remember the street lights on Sangamon Street changing from gas to electric. Milk, as well as ice, was delivered in horse-drawn wagons. Our milkman delivered Wanzer products in a green truck or wagon, and I remember the slogan "Wanzer on milk is like sterling on silver." An old black man we called "the junk man" came around in a horse-drawn wagon. He would call out, "Rags and iron, babies for sale!" A guy we called "the vegetable man" also came around in an old truck. And then there was "The Good Humor Man" in his white uniform who sold ice cream bars from his white truck.

It seems that as far back as I can remember, all the way through high school years, we often went to Grandma Celia Olson's house for Sunday dinner. The Ed Sullivan Show was always the climax of the evening. These family get-togethers always included my mother's aunt, Hulda Bjorn, Hulda's daughter, Marion, and Bill Sallay, Marion's husband. This was the nucleus of our family.

Bill Sallay, Hulda Bjorn, and Marion. We were very close.

We saw my mother's brother, Uncle Roger Olson and his family, perhaps once a year as they lived in California. My father's mother, Grandma Annette Guentner, who remarried Frank Guentner, came to visit from Oklahoma City perhaps once a year.

First Cousins – Becky Olson, Nancy Olson,
Janet Wiltz, Roger Wiltz, John Wiltz

Frank and Grandma Annette Guentner

I sometimes look back and measure time by what the family car was. Perhaps it's a guy thing. I was about five when Dad and I went down the block after supper and bought a neighbor's 1939 LaSalle. It didn't run, and we towed it to our driveway with a chain. Dad got it running, and I can remember a Christmas vacation trip to Florida in that car. To my brother and me, that backseat was as big as a playroom. I also remember getting carsick in the Ozarks and puking into one of dad's rubber galoshes.

In 1951, Grandma Olson, who had some money, bought our family and my Uncle Roger's family a new car. I was privileged to go along when both cars were purchased. Uncle Olie and Aunt Frances bought a very sharp Oldsmobile two-door coupe, and Dad bought a Hudson Commodore-Six four-door.

Our new 1951 Hudson. Left to right - sister Janet, Roger, brother John, and neighbor Chucky Trisko.

Now a bit about immediate family. On April 12, 1942, I was born in the Little Company of Mary Hospital in Evergreen Park, IL, a nearby Chicago suburb. John Byron followed me on June 26, 1944, Janet Cecelia on September 19, 1948, and Michael David on June 26, 1956.

John Byron Wiltz, Roger Allan Wiltz

The Wiltz kids - Mike, John, Janet, Roger

Nancy Olson, John L. Wiltz, Janet Wiltz

My mother, Lucille Ireta Olson, was born in Chicago on November 24, 1916. John Leonard Wiltz, my father, was born on October 19, 1911, in Peoria, IL. I knew both of my grandmothers well, but both grandfathers died before I was born. Leo Wiltz was killed in a Chicago grain elevator explosion in 1921, and John Algot Olson died from an appendicitis in 1935.

John and Lucille's wedding day. Nov. 1937

On my father's side, Peter Wilz, a schoolmaster at Michelbach, Bavaria, married Eva Gertrude Huth. They came to America on the Holland where their 8th child, Michael, was born at sea. They settled at Lourdes, IL, about 5 miles west of Metamora in 1836. Their children were Henry (dob 12/5/18), John, Eve, Adad, Peter, Lawrence, Gertrude, and the afore-mentioned Michael.

At age 18, Henry Wilz, my great great grandfather, decided to stay in the Cincinnati area. At 29 yrs. of age, Henry enlisted in the army joining Company A of the 4th Ohio Volunteer Regiment. After seeing heavy action in the Mexican War, he mustered out of the army on 7/22/1848. I find it interesting that in looking at Henry's regiment losses, four were killed in battle, one died later from wounds, and 71 died from disease. A very lucky Henry married Anna Weis in Cincinnati on 12/6/49.

They had 7 children. At the age of 43, prompted by the Civil War, Henry again joined the army on 9/1/61. His outfit was the 44th Illinois Company K. He left his wife, Anna, who was 8 months pregnant, with 6 children. Frank, the 7th, was born on 10/10/61 in Peoria, IL.

Peoria, IL. Front: Helen, baby Rita, great grandma Fischer, great grandma Wiltz. Back: John Wiltz, great grandpa Frank Wiltz

Frank Wiltz, was my great grandfather, and I remember him and his wife, Mary Stoehr Wiltz, living in Champaign, IL in an upstairs apartment above my great aunt, Clara Walk. Frank and Mary had 3 children – Oliver, Leo, and Clara Anna.

grandpa Leo Wiltz

Leo Wiltz, my grandfather, married Annette Fischer. They had 3 children – Helen, John Leonard Wiltz, my father, and Rita. Neither of my aunts married or had children. For those interested, I have very detailed information on the Wilz or Wiltz family.

**Rita Wiltz on 5/23/43 as bridesmaid. Rita never came out
of anesthesia during cosmetic surgery on her nose**

On my mother's side, my grandfather, John Algot Olson, was born in Sunne, Sweden on 2/20/1885. My maternal grandmother, Celia Bjorn Olson, was born in Chicago on 1/13/1886. They had 2 children – my mother, Lucille Ireta Olson, and my uncle, Roger Algot Olson. I remember my maternal great grandparents, John Algot and Tillie, but I am not familiar with their history.

Seated: Lucille, my mother, & Roger, my uncle. Standing:
Grandfather John Algot, Grandmother Celia

Great Grandmother Tillie, Great Grandfather
John Algot, Grandmother Celia

My uncle, baby Roger Olson & Great Grandfather John Algot Olson – founder of Standard Sash & Door Company

Grandmother Celia and baby Roger

My Grandma Celia's mother was an interesting, if not prolific, character. Emma Eckstrom was born in Helsingborg (Skona) Sweden on 10/10/1864. She married Charles Bjorn in 1882 and gave birth to six children including my grandmother, Celia Bjorn. Charles died in 1891, and Emma remarried Peter Horslev in 1899.

They had three children. I remember Great Grandma Horslev telling me that Abe Lincoln once held her hand when she was an infant.

Cedar Lake, Indiana was a part of "My Chicago." My maternal grandmother's summer cottage in a subdivision on the east side of the lake had been in the Olson family since the mid 1920's. The lake cottage was about thirty miles southeast of our Chicago home.

The Fishbaugh family owned a cottage in the neighboring Hickory subdivision, and my father's boyhood friend, Bob Fishbaugh, often invited my father to visit. My mother met my father at Cedar Lake in the 1920's.

Bob and Harriet Fishbaugh, my parents Lucille & John Wiltz in Chicago night club 6/21/53

If you read, *They Said It Couldn't Be Done: The Incredible Story of Bill Lear* by author Victor Boesen, you will learn that on a backyard swing at that Cedar Lake summer cottage, my grandfather, John Algot Olson, loaned Bill Lear five-thousand dollars. Lear wanted to develop a coil for automobile radios, but he couldn't get the funding for development. Lear's coil spawned the birth of the Motorola Incorporated. Grandad believed in Lear when others didn't, and you know the rest of the Lear Jet story. John Algot Olson was president of Chicago's Standard Sash and Door Company.

**My fisherman grandfather John Algot Olson,
the man who financed Bill Lear**

Most of my summers, with the exception of the ones where I played baseball with the Oakdale Park Babe Ruth League, were spent at Cedar Lake. While working my summer jobs during my college years, I often drove to the lake after work. So did my father, and so did my brother, John Byron.

We, my brothers, sister, and I, learned to fish at Cedar Lake off of the subdivision pier. With bobbers and worms we caught bluegills and perch. A night crawler on the bottom caught big bullheads. The first small perch of the day would swim beneath a big bobber with a hook through his back. Usually he caught nothing, but sometimes a pike, bass, or big dogfish would grab him and the fight was on! We learned much of this from Mom.

Once I had a driver's license, it was off to the drive-in movie theatre in Cook. Two bodies lay on the backseat floor under a rug. Four more might fit in the trunk. Creativity was the only limitation as the girls had just as much fun as the guys!

Cedar Lake also meant shopping trips to Crown Point with its Lake County fair grounds and covered bridge. Crown Point was also home of the Lake County jail where John Dillinger made his famous escape. We had mom repeat that story a hundred times.

When I was about eight or nine, dad brought me along to the golf course to pull his cart. It wasn't long before he let me whack at a ball between holes, and within a short time I received a set of clubs as a birthday gift.

The Cedar Lake South Shore Golf Club was a mile south of our subdivision road. We carried our clubs to the course, and they allowed, actually encouraged, us kids to golf free on weekdays. A day didn't pass without golfing at least 18 holes. I remember breaking 80 with a 79 on the par 72 course before I graduated from high school, and in those days they didn't have the shorter weenie tee boxes in front of the men's tees. Monday morning was always reserved for looking for balls after the busy weekend, and there was a time I had hundreds of golf balls. The names Titleist, Acushnet, Spaulding, Wilson, Po-Do, and Dunlap come to mind.

Golf became very important to me, and somewhere in the rafters of the garage are a box of golf trophies. I still golf today. My Chicago was a very special place.

Good Times

My Chicago was a magnificent place to grow up. Always there was something to see or do, and my parents utilized those opportunities to the fullest. If mom or dad needed a break on Sundays, it never showed.

Often I've heard it said that we inner city dwellers didn't know our neighbors. We knew our Sangamon Street neighbors and called them by name. We also depended on one another like country people. During the summer there were block parties. Charcoal grills dotted the street as the smoky aroma of burgers, brats, and wieners permeated the air, an air filled with music.

Christmases were a ritual. Our tree went up on Christmas Eve afternoon. By this time tree selection was limited, but that didn't matter to Dad as he was looking for a bargain. Gaping holes were easily filled by drilling holes and inserting the extra loose branches we garnered. The end result was a perfect tree. We opened gifts on early Christmas Day morning before mass at St. Margaret's.

The earliest Christmas Eves I can remember were at Great Grandpa and Grandma Olson's three-flat apartment house on south Eberhart Street. With their passing Christmas Eve moved to Grandma Olson's on Aberdeen Street.

It was a festive occasion that included Great Grandma and Grandpa Olson, Grandma Olson, my mother's aunts and uncles Art and Marie, Bernard and Cleo, and Walter and Violet. Art and Marie's daughters

Jeannie and Sandra were there, along with my Uncle Olie (Roger Olson) and Aunt Frances. Their daughters, Nancy and Becky, would soon join us. My mother's aunts, Hulda and Mildred, were present, along with my mother's cousin Marion and her boyfriend Bill. Our family rounded out the celebration. Uncle Olie played Santa Claus, something I didn't figure out right away. All of the above family information has been reinforced in my memory by old 16 mm movies that I have put on a modern CD.

The singular Christmas gift I well remember from my earliest days was built by my father for my brother and me. Mom and Dad called it "The Electronic Toy." It was a large battery-powered plywood box with switches and buttons for flashing red, white, and blue lights, sirens, bells, and buzzers. The making of Christmas gifts filtered down to my brother and me as we made jigsaw puzzles by gluing pictures onto plywood or Masonite and cutting them into intricate pieces on the jigsaw.

In the early spring dad took us kids to the lake front where we netted smelt by the carload. I can remember a trunk full of smelt and a backseat filled to the back of the front seat with smelt. Neighbors waited for our arrival home – sometimes at one or two in the morning. Then we sat in a circle on folding chairs and pails cleaning smelt 'til dawn with a scissors in hand. A grill was fired up, and we munched on crispy smelt as we snipped off the head, snipped open the belly, and flicked out the guts. Believe it or not, those smelt smelled like watermelon. Everyone went home with a bag-full of fresh smelt.

Some good things have been lost over the years, and kite flying is certainly one of them. I just don't see kids flying kites anymore. Perhaps the dads who built them are gone.

Dad was a master kite builder. He built different models, but box kites might have been his favorite. He also made this giant wooden reel that held hundreds of yards of kite string. At the time, the 9500 block of

Sangamon Street was void of houses, and the whole block-long field was clear of power and telephone lines. It was kite heaven. If the wind was too strong and the kite difficult to control, we added lengths of tail. As I write this today, I wonder if my grandkids are too old to enjoy a kite.

We often went to grandma's house for Sunday dinner, but if we didn't, it was because of a family outing. We could count on going somewhere every Sunday after church. Winter destinations included The Museum of Science & Industry as well as the Field Museum of Natural History with its mummies. I had a strong interest in archeology.

Astronomy was becoming a borderline passion, and the Adler Planetarium was a favorite. The same was true of the Shedd Aquarium as fish were always special. As little tots, we immensely enjoyed trips to Midway where we watched the airplanes land and takeoff through a large glass window. The zoos, Lincoln Park and Brookfield, were also frequent favorites. Bushman, a gorilla, was a Lincoln Park institution.

Madison Street's old Chicago Stadium was the site of a circus that brings back two very clear memories, one of which terrorized me at the time. I must have been about nine-years-old. I remember mom and dad being there, but I don't know about my brother. My first vivid memory is that of standing in front of Hopalong Cassidy's horse, Topper, after the performance was over. The horse was immense, but Hopalong, Bill Boyd, didn't seem all that big.

My second recollection was frightening. The circus performance ended when a large cannon, mounted on the back of a truck with the barrel pointed forward over the cab, rolled into the corner of the arena. A line of people walked in a circle around the cannon truck, and one of them would be chosen to be fired from the cannon. Finally the ill-fated candidate climbed up and slid down into the barrel. Following a drumroll, the cannon roared, and the victim sailed through the air across the arena floor and landed in a big net. For a time I feared all guns and especially the noise they produced, but I did get over it as dad introduced us to gun handling, target practice, and ultimately hunting.

As we grew older, the Harding Museum with its extensive collection of antique firearms was popular with dad, my brother, and me. The last time I saw the Harding collection, it was in the basement of the Chicago Art Institute. I can also remember touring palace-like mansions along Lake Shore Drive before they were demolished.

Summer weekends were often spent at grandma's Cedar Lake, Indiana summer cottage. It must have been in the early summer before school was out that dad took us to Wrigley Field or Comiskey Park for a Cubs or White Sox Game. I've seen the great Jackie Robinson, but I had no particular appreciation for the man back then. I also hated his Dodgers as they were hard on my Cubs.

Though we lived on the South Side, and the White Sox were the South Side team, I became a Cubs fan. It seems I've led a life of being a contrary devil's advocate. The Cubs have been known as "Loveable Losers," and those are the Cubs I knew as a youth. A .500 won-loss record was bliss. Hank "Sauer the Power" played left field, and player-manager Phil Cavarretta often pinch-hit. One could be a Wrigley Field bleacher bum for fifty cents in those days.

By far, the high point of my 7th, 8th, and 9th grade summers was baseball in the Oakdale Park Babe Ruth League for 13-15 year olds. I'm quite sure it was tailored for the graduates of the highly popular Little League, and I sweated over surviving the tryouts and making the cut as I hadn't been a Little League grad.

Though I was very clumsy as a result of growing tall too quickly, I could "bring it" with my 6'4" frame as far as throwing the ball was concerned, and I wound up being the six-team league's all-star first baseman as well as a respectable pitcher.

Baseball was an important confidence builder for me, and I owe our coach, Mr. Jerry Mulderink, for shaping a group of boys with no particular talent into a well-oiled team by practicing every day. We were league champs three years running. To this day I don't know who paid for the uniforms, bases, bats, balls, and umpire equipment. Dad was a highly respected league umpire. What I remember most was being a pitcher and not being able to get a called third strike if the game depended on it.

As previously mentioned, Oakdale Park was where you found me after school. We chose up sides and played baseball, football (always tackle), and hockey in season. The park featured a fieldhouse and activities director, Tony Fonfara. We thought the world of Tony. He tried to teach us to square dance, wrestle, and build models. We could also checkout equipment, bats, and balls with Tony. He wasn't a regular, but on occasion, Dick Butkus was part of the group. Butkus went on to be a Chicago Bears great.

When Grandma Guentner, my father's mother, made her annual visit to Chicago from Oklahoma City, she always took me downtown on the Rock Island commuter train to the LaSalle Street Station. From there we walked. Marshall Fields was a certain destination. So was lunch at either The Berghoff, a German restaurant, or the Chinese restaurant, Hoe Sai Gai. Always we went to the afternoon movie matinee at The Chicago Theatre where a singular performance stands out in my memory.

The movie feature, "This is Cinerama," didn't particularly impress me. What did impress me was the on stage performance by black vocalist and pianist, Nat King Cole. The man's talent captivated me.…... something that doesn't often happen to a ten-year-old. I didn't know who Cole was until that day, but I've never forgotten him since. Today I ask myself why someone of Cole's stature was playing second fiddle to a movie matinee. The year was 1952, and Nat King Cole was a celebrity.

By high school graduation in 1960, I had become increasingly interested in girls. Up until that point, I had been on three dates with the opposite sex. Two of the three were my junior and senior prom. I believe that attending an all-boys high school had in part slowed my social development as far as girls were concerned.

My first ever date came about in the middle of my junior year when Mary, a grade school classmate, invited me to a dance at her high school, Academy of Our Lady. I hadn't seen Mary in two-and-a-half years, and I don't know that I had ever talked to her when we were classmates at St. Margaret's grade school. When she called, I asked my mom what I should do while Mary waited on the phone. Mom replied, "You go to the dance." Some dance lessons from mom followed immediately. I certainly had zero for social skills. A second result of Mary's invitation was the acquisition of a driver's license.

As it turned out, I did enjoy the dance, and I did like Mary. I mostly remember the nuns cruising around the dance floor and separating couples that were dancing too closely together in their estimation. At my parent's urging, I reciprocated by inviting Mary to my junior prom.

Date wise, doing something special became important to me, and Chicago certainly offered some special attractions. Riverview and Ravinia Park were among my favorite destinations, and to my way of thinking, Riverview was the world's premier amusement park.

The Bobs, what has been acclaimed as the greatest rollercoaster of all time, was perhaps the most famous Riverview attraction. Other than four additional awesome rollercoasters, The Shoot the Chutes, The Tunnel of Love, The Rotor, and the parachute all bring fond memories. At Riverview, one could remain on a ride and go again for pennies.

The Rotor was a large enclosure shaped like a one-pound coffee can. As it rotated, the floor fell out and centrifugal force held one against the side wall. Though I easily get motion sickness, a young lady once talked me into going on the rotor with her. It was ugly. When I threw-up, the vomit suspended in the air in front of me before splashing back into my face.

Ravinia Park was a beautiful insect-free park of lush grass and stately trees in a concert setting of central stage and state of the art sound system. One could spread a blanket wherever one wished and lay or sit back with beverages of choice.

If I were to narrow all my life's entertainment experiences down to a single pleasurable event, I would choose the night we spread a blanket in front of the stage that featured Louis "Satchmo" Armstrong in person. Never has one entertainer enthralled an audience the way Armstrong did that night. When that white handkerchief came out, electricity flowed through the air. Curtain calls followed curtain calls. The man was ultimately exhausted.

School Days

St. Margaret's Elementary

Considering I was six-years-old at the time, I find my recall rather amazing. Mom and I made the near mile walk to St. Margaret of Scotland Catholic elementary school at 99th Street and Throop. When we entered the 1st grade classroom, the sight of that nun in the School Sisters of Notre Dame black and white habit must have terrorized me. I was throwing a screaming tantrum when Sister Lucy told my mother to leave and that everything would be just fine. In looking back, it must have been more difficult for mom than it was for me.

Through the eight years, the day usually began with mass at 8:00 a.m. although it wasn't mandatory. By fifth grade we were part of the choir that sang the Kyrie, Gloria, Credo, Sanctus, and Agnus Dei in Latin. I can still remember the chanted lyrics.

It was during my first grade year that I was being bullied by an older boy, a third grader, on my way home after school. Tommy, the bully, lived on the 9600 block of Morgan Street, the first street west of Sangamon. Mom wanted to meet with his parents. Dad wanted me to fight back. I was very meek and timid. I wanted mom's intervention, and I didn't know if I had the courage to fight back as dad instructed.

The next time I was about to be pushed around, I swung at the boy with my lunch box. It was a heavy metal box my father had used during the war, not one of those with Gene Autry's picture on the side. The box struck his mouth, breaking his upper front teeth off at the gum line. The bully headed home bleeding and crying. I feared the front door bell was going to ring that night.

As anticipated, the bell rang. Tommy, his mom, and his dad were at the door. When I explained what had happened and why, they said, "Thank-you" and left. That was the last we heard of the matter.

Probably because I loathed school, it was difficult. Some summer school reading work was required for promotion to the fourth grade. I remember the typical and hated motivational incentives. During the season, every student had his/her own construction paper Thanksgiving turkey, Christmas tree, or Easter basket with their name on the bulletin board. When some good work was done, the turkey received a feather, the tree gained an ornament, or the basket displayed a new egg. My turkey was nude, my tree was bare, and my basket was empty.

Then there were the dreaded reading groups. I especially despised the apple-polishing girls in the "Blue Bird" group. The "Robins" made up the middle group, and the "Crows" brought up the rear. I was a crow, and I saw myself doomed to crowdom for life.

I remember sitting around in a circle with the guys during lunch hour and talking about what our dads did in the war. Killing Japs and Nazis, manning destroyers and aircraft carriers, and bombing raids over Germany were often told stories. My father wasn't in the war, and I kept my mouth shut. I didn't realize that seven days a week of B-29 production in the Chrysler plant was just as important. But when the talk came around to "my dad could whip your dad," then I spoke my piece.

Any playground talk of sex must have been strictly taboo as it never happened. The closest we came to sex talk was the color of underpants different girls were wearing, and this was easily determined with a trip to the swings or monkey bars. In the primary grades, the girls wore blue jumpers and white blouses, and we wore blue trousers, white shirts, and blue ties. The attire became more liberalized in the later years.

A first ray of promise was revealed in the early days of 4th grade. As a composition assignment, we were to write about something that happened during the summer. My brother and I had caught a very large perch while staying at my grandmother's summer cottage at Cedar Lake, Indiana, and we decided to mount it. We nailed it to a board, painted it, and hung it on the wall.

As the perch mellowed, it became increasingly offensive to Grandma Olson and Aunt Hulda. They scrubbed and scrubbed to no avail, but it only became worse. When they asked Byron and me about the odor, we suggested it might be the fish they hadn't seen on the wall by the sailboat. Sister Patricia Ann was beside herself in laughter, and she read the composition to the entire class.

5th grade saw my education turn in a very positive direction. Miss Catherine Clinton was my teacher, and I soon found myself liking school. A second good thing was also happening. I began taking accordion lessons as a 4th grader, and I was often asked to bring the accordion to school. I thrived on the attention.

Miss Clinton was also the indirect cause of the most trouble I had ever encountered. At the time, 1952, a popular TV-radio jingle went, "HFC – Household Finance Corporation." On the school yard I heard some older boy say, "HFC – Horse Face Clinton!" I popped him in the nose, and he went down hard. I loved that old woman. I was soon in the principal's office, and mom and dad were called to school. Promises were made, there was some Saturday school in the convent lobby, and I was never in trouble again – at least grade school trouble.

A defining point in my personal confidence also happened during my 5th grade year. About a thousand of us were in the church on a Friday afternoon, and a visiting priest was giving us a lecture on the subject of mortal sin. Toward the end of his presentation, he asked all of us to stand up. He then instructed us to sit down when his descriptions of sin had reached mortal sin status.

It seems a boy stole various items from the five and dime store. A few kids sat down. This continued and a few more of my peers sat down. One thing led to another, and he eventually lied to his mother when she asked where the goods came from. More like transgressions followed, and in the end, I was the last student standing. The nuns were glaring at me.

"What's your name, son?" the priest asked.

"Roger," I quivered.

"Why are you standing?" inquired the priest.

"Because ten venial sins don't make a mortal sin," I answered.

"Roger, you are correct!" blurted father. I believe from that point on, my classmates and the nuns viewed me in a new light.

At some point during this time period, I smoked my first and only cigarette ever behind the school incinerators during the lunch hour. We were inspired by some western movie where Alan Ladd or Randolph Scott had rolled a cigarette while riding a horse across the open range. I had acquired a five-cent cloth pouch of Bull Durham tobacco and a little packet of Zig-Zag papers.

We poured tobacco onto the paper, wet the edges with a tongue, and rolled them into the ugliest cigarettes ever created. I lit up, inhaled, and nearly gaged to death. It was the last puff of tobacco I ever drew save the one time I tried a pipe during my college years.

As a 6th grader, I must have missed school on the day we were taught how to multiply decimals. We were given a multiplication test the following day. Four and five-digit decimals were multiplied by each other. I had no idea whatsoever what to do with the decimals other than guess. When Sister Cornelius returned the exams, she was angry. No one had scored a perfect paper. She then went on to say that in spite of the fact that one boy had done all the math correctly, he failed to get one correct answer.

Sister then called me to the blackboard where she asked me to do a few of the problems. When the math work was completed less the decimals, she guided my hand to the blackboard and proceeded to count off places behind the decimals with my hand. She then counted off the same number of places from right to left in the answer and smacked down the decimal point. While there may have been a less embarrassing way to teach me the process, I never made a decimal mistake again so far as I know.

The 7th grade highlight of the year was the 7th & 8th grade trip to Washington D.C. The cost was fifty dollars, a great deal of money in the spring of 1955. When I asked mom and dad if I could go, they said we couldn't afford it. I was heartbroken, but I accepted it. That night I overheard mom and dad discussing it in bed. Mom was talking about how badly I wanted to go. In the morning they told me I could go! What made it all the better was that my best friend, David Trisko, was also going. We would be D.C. hotel roommates with the Spingola brothers.

The Sisters of Notre Dame were master teachers. They made high school and college easy for me. Fractions and sentence diagramming were not negotiable items. Their discipline and command for respect were absolute. In eight years, I never heard a student get smart-mouthed with a teacher. It was always, "Yes, sister!" More amazing, there were fifty students in a classroom.

ST MARGARET
SCHOOL
GRADE 6
ROOM 17
SEPT 28 1953

Every nun had at least 50 students

It troubles me when I hear of physical abuse by nuns. I was never smacked across the knuckles with a ruler, and I never witnessed such activity. The closest thing to abuse I can remember was being led from the classroom by the ear. They loved God, and they cared deeply for their students. They were also clouded in mystery. None of us could ever recall a sister taking a restroom break.

The train for D.C. left Chicago on Friday afternoon. We arrived in Washington Saturday morning, and the tour began. After mass in the Cathredral Sunday morning, we were back on the train after a group photo in front of the capitol. We had school on Monday.

I'll never forget Friday night on the train. The porters announced that we could rent a pillow for twenty-five cents. Dale Deats was the class clown. He also had money, and he was going to be our hero. Dale was going to corner the market on pillows. By doing so, none of the sisters would have a pillow. What a plan! We guys were giggling with anticipation. Dale's seat was piled high with pillows. About 8:30 p.m., Sister Clarona, the principal, came up to Dale.

"Dale, we sisters will have our pillows now."

"Yes Sister!" Dale responded. Some hero. So much for the great pillow caper.

8th grade was a wonderful but stressful year. Sister Enid understood adolescent teens. She could be one of us as she excelled in our softball games over the lunch hour. She danced to "In the Mood" when I played it on my accordion. I later realized that she was probably a teen during Glen Miller's heyday although a nun's age was an oft discussed unknown quantity in our eyes.

It was during the 8th grade year that I assumed some major responsibility. I was a patrol boy. We patrol boys worked busy intersections before and after school by going out into the street, stopping traffic, and signaling for students to cross. We wore a white diagonal belt attached to a waist belt. That belt was rolled in a particular manner and hung from our waist when we were off-duty. To us patrol boys, it was a badge of honor and courage. We were fortunate that none of us were ever killed while on duty. My beat was 99th and Vincennes – one of the busiest.

As 8th graders, we had to decide where we were going to high school unless we chose public school. Most of us would go to a catholic school, and most of the girls went to the nearby Academy of Our Lady on 95th Street. For boys the decision wasn't so easy. Brother Rice, the new Christian Brothers high school on Pulaski, was a popular choice. So was St. Rita, Leo, Mt. Carmel, and Mendel. All required a Saturday morning entrance exam, and acceptance was far from a sure thing. Fortunately I had my choice, and I really can't remember why I chose Mendel Catholic. Perhaps it was closest.

In looking back at the eight years of St. Margaret's, the sisters would break up the routine from time to time. In June 1953, a television set was brought into the classroom to cover Queen Elizabeth's coronation. Occasionally a 16 mm projector was set up in the afternoon to show a movie. In particular I remember "The Five Sullivans," and I can still remember Thomas Mitchell waving at his sons from the train. More than once the sisters marched us to the Beverly Theatre on 95th and Ashland Ave. for a movie. "The Robe" and "Quo Vatis" come to mind.

In March of 1953 I was sitting in a 5th grade classroom when Sister Clarona announced over the PA (public address system) that Joseph Stalin was dead. There was an air of satisfaction, and I couldn't imagine nuns being grateful for anyone's death.

During the summer of 1956, the summer between 8th grade graduation and the beginning of high school at Mendel, the John Kilgallon family from the East Side of Chicago bought a summer cottage on Cedar Lake, IN. It was in the same subdivision as my grandmother's summer cottage, and Don Kilgallon and I became close friends. Don, who would be a sophomore at Mendel, was invaluable as a mentor who got me started on the right foot. He was eventually the best man at my wedding, and I at his.

Mendel Catholic High School

Mendel Catholic High School, located at 250 East Indiana Ave., was approximately three-and-a-half miles southeast of our home. During good weather, I sometimes walked or rode my bike to school. Most of the time I walked down to 96th & Halsted and boarded a CTA (Chicago Transit Authority) bus that brought me to 111th and Halsted. I then transferred onto a 111th street bus and exited at Mendel's front gate.

Mendel, an all-boys school run by Augustinian priests, was the former Pullman Free School of Manual Training, a private school for the children of Pullman railroad car employees. The sprawling campus featured a lake in the shape of a "P" in front of the main entrance.

Mendel Campus – note "P"-shaped lake

During the years I attended Mendel (1956-1960), the enrollment was approximately 1600 students. The curriculum was college prep although there was a metal shop. At our ten-year reunion, I learned that 90% of my fellow grads had earned a master's degree or beyond. While most of the classroom teachers were priests, there were some lay teachers.

In spite of the rigid discipline, I loved that school. We maintained silence in the halls and rose when an adult entered the room. Detentions or "jug" were administered freely by the staff, and that meant showing up at 7:00 a.m. the following morning and reporting to a one-time coal bin in the basement to copy grammar rules from an ancient text with paper and pencil. One didn't skip "jug."

During my senior year I picked up a detention. The wrestling team was to head to Milwaukee the following morning to wrestle Pius XI, and I saw myself as a valuable member of the squad. When I told Father Pazera that I'd be missing detention in the morning as I was a member of the wrestling team, he told me to keep going if I missed "jug." I went to detention, and I never told Mom or Dad about it. Could you imagine this happening today?

Speaking of Father Pazera, he would come into a classroom with his hair clippers and extension cord. We were to sit up straight and face the front. No one dared look back. He approached from the rear. When the footsteps stopped and the clippers turned on, someone whose hair was too long to suit him was going to lose a swath of hair right down the middle. There were no DA (duck ass) haircuts at Mendel.

To my knowledge there was no corporal punishment at Mendel, but there was physical pain. In physics lab, when Father Burke said, "Mr. Wiltz, kneel out," it meant kneeling on your fingers for the remainder of the period. That got old in a hurry.

There was also "Nickel Nose." That amounted to holding a nickel against the wall with one's nose while hands were held behind the back. If the nickel fell, more time was added. It once bought a laugh from friends when I had the image of a buffalo (buffalo nickel) imprinted on the end of my nose. During my early days of classroom teaching, I used "Nickel Nose" effectively. While The Jug, Kneeling Out, and Nickel Nose seem harsh by today's standards, our current schools would be so much more effective with some old time discipline supported by old time parenting.

Remembering particular classes is difficult, but I do remember Father Durant's sophomore speech and composition class. In order to familiarize us with gestures, he taught us Shakespearian gestures, and had us memorize a scene from *The Merchant of Venice.* He believed that by having each of us perform that scene, any gestures to follow would come easily.

The drill was effective, and I used the same exercise in speech classes I taught. This past summer I was invited to a 50th class reunion at Willow Lake, SD where I first taught. I was stunned when one of the girls, a life-long teacher herself, began performing that same speech. It is said that a teacher's influence is eternal as we never know where that influence stops. Father Durant was alive and well in Willow Lake, and I can still deliver that speech.

Father Durant required a weekly composition. On the due day, we would lay the composition on our desk tops. He would walk up and down the isles and inspect each composition for 10-15 seconds. If he spotted a spelling error or sentence fragment, the piece was crumpled up, and zero credit was given. We learned quickly.

Father Hennessey taught Algebra II. Day after day the drill was the same.

"Mr. Wiltz come to the board and do problem six. We call Mr. Wiltz 'Sonny' because he's so bright. We have him do the problem because he will cover every possible problem along the way." In spite of the seeming ridicule, I loved that old man.

During the fall of 1957, Mendel won the Chicago City Football Championship played in front of over 100,000 fans at Soldiers Field. The game featured the Catholic League Champions vs. the Public School Champions, the Calumet Indians. The Mendel Monarchs won 6-0 on a final second "Hail Mary" pass to the end zone.

I will never forget the Friday afternoon before the Saturday game. The old building literally rocked as 1600 students pounded their feet while chanting, "Have no pity, we want city!" Over 40 fan buses lined up on the campus the following morning. Football became a very big deal.

Along with 900 other Mendel men, I tried out for the football team the following spring. Mats were spread out on the gym floor. Coaches McGee and Novak called out two of our names. We were to face each other from opposite sides of the mat. When the whistle blew, we charged each other. Short of fists, it was "anything goes." If one or both flinched on impact, they were thanked and dismissed.

When the new recruits were whittled down to thirty, football gear was checked out for a full month of spring drills. When this group was thinned out to 15-20, they joined the returning team for another month of spring football. I and a few others were permitted to miss an occasional day of spring football for track meets. In the Catholic League, I finished second in city in the shot put that spring.

Two football incidents come to mind. During a one-on-one drill, Coach McGee asked why everyone was afraid of Ed. Ed Burke would go on to play for Notre Dame and the Houston Oilers. I walked over to Ed, gave him a shove, and called him "dog puke." Ed was beside himself. Coach McGee lined us up nose to nose. When Ed struck me across the face, he blackened both eyes, broke my nose, and knocked me cold. I can still hear McGee saying, "Wiltz, get up!" though I couldn't move a muscle.

I never made the starting lineup until the particular fall Sunday afternoon when Coach McGee came up to me during warmups and asked, "Wiltz, where were you last night?"

"Home with my family watching 'Gun Smoke,'" I responded. While we dressed for the game it had been rumored that some of the guys had gotten into trouble.

"You're starting at right tackle today. No matter what I call you or say to you today, stay in the game," spoke McGee. I stayed in the game, but I didn't perform very well.

It was halftime when Coach Novak led me into the shower room and asked, "Wiltz, what can you do on defense that you can't do on offense?"

"Use my hands!" I responded.

"Right, Wiltz! Do you know how?" asked Novak?

"I think I know how," I answered.

"Like this!" yelled Novak as he shoved a hand into my mouth. The insides of both my upper and lower lips were shredded against my teeth. I spit blood onto the shower room floor as Novak walked out. I stayed in the game, but never started another game. I never had a problem with Coach Novak's lesson. As a coach years later I realized that I lacked the lateral movement necessary for that level of play.

1958 Mendel Monarchs. I'm #46

In the Chicago Catholic League, the basketball teams were made up of two equally important varsity teams – The Lights and The Heavies. To qualify as a Light, one had to be no taller than 5'8". There was an official pre-season "measure-in," and I can remember some of the guys trying to remain on their feet for 48 hours. Apparently the body would compress if they could stand long enough. Mendel won the Lights Catholic League City Championship in 1959.

Toward the end of winter during my junior year, I was an intramural wrestling champion at 185 pounds. Intramural sports were big at Mendel, and the 1959 intramural champs formed the nucleus of the new interscholastic wrestling team that took to the mat in 1959-1960. Both my brother and I made the starting lineup for Coach Lou Guida. It was good times!

I was vice-president of the Mendel archeology club during my junior year. We made a field trip to the St. Anne, IL area to look for Indian artifacts, and my brother, also a member, and I decided to take our .22 rifles along. Why Father Burke, our adviser, allowed this I'll never know. I'll also never know how I could have been that stupid.

During the expedition, we spent part of the time in Forest Preserve where firearms were illegal, and it was soon discovered. J.B. and I were given citations and our rifles were confiscated. A court appearance was scheduled for the following Saturday morning. As it turned out, we were fined fifteen dollars apiece and our rifles were returned to us. Dad surprisingly said very little about it.

Months later on Christmas morning there were envelopes for Byron and me under the tree. Money! I happily thought. I was very wrong. The envelopes held the fifteen dollar receipts from the court appearance. Today it's a fond memory.

The junior prom was in the school gym. The senior prom was in the ballroom of a downtown hotel. The good fathers warned us that if a prom dress was too revealing, the young lady would be handed a Mendel sweatshirt. Father O'Rourke was at the door with a box of sweatshirts. I believe that Guy Lombardo played the music for our senior prom. If I recall, we paid a fifteen dollar fee for music and prom banquet – a lot of money in 1960.

Back then the seniors had a smoking lounge, a privilege that was often revoked. I personally found the room disgusting as I hated cigarettes, a feeling that was nurtured by too many trips to the corner store to buy cigarettes for my parents. One had difficulty seeing across that smoking room.

Mendel was famous for its Sunday night sock hops. The gym was always packed, and the stands were literally packed with shoes as we danced in our stocking feet! I can remember when the student senate told Father McNabb, the senate adviser, that our own Peter Cetera was good enough to do the music on Sunday night. Indeed he was as the whole world can attest to! (Chicago)

I don't know how many defining moments come along in one's life, but I certainly experienced one toward the end of wrestling season during my senior year. Lou Guida, our coach, asked me if I planned to go to college. I answered "yes" as my parents let me know early on that college wasn't an option. Dad also wanted me to be an engineer. I had already been accepted at The University of Dayton as my best friend, Don Kilgallon, went to Dayton.

Coach Guida mentioned South Dakota State, his alma mater, and offered to take me to the campus for the weekend of the spring training alumni football game. I don't know if I knew where South Dakota was, but I did know there were lots of pheasants from reading outdoor magazines. In the end, I chose South Dakota State for all the wrong reasons – one of the most fortunate decisions of my life.

Thanks to Coach Guida, I had a room in Gym Dorm and a job in the athletic offices that paid my board. Though I wasn't a good football player, I was good enough to make a squad that won consecutive North Central championships. Coach Guida put a lot of pressure on me, and one didn't disappoint Coach Guida. I was the first from Mendel. If I kept my nose clean, kept up my grades, and made the squad, others from Mendel could follow. Two great Mendel Monarchs followed – Tackle Dennis Dee and Quarterback Pat Durkin.

In wrapping up my four years at Mendel, it was an easy trek after school or football practice up to "The Ave" or Michigan Avenue. It was "the thing" to do. Walgreen's sat on the southwest corner of 111th and Michigan, and a nickel bought a Coke or cherry phosphate at the marble soda fountain. State Street was another block west, and that offered White Castle hamburgers for 12 cents apiece. Life was good.

Hobbies and Pass-times

At some point during my 4th grade year, I began to take accordion lessons. I really don't know how this came about, but my parents encouraged it as my mother and uncle could both play the piano. The accordion lessons continued into my high school years, and I became at least respectable on the squeeze box. On occasion teachers asked me to bring it to school, and I'll give the accordion credit for giving me some much needed self-confidence. I won't call myself a professional musician, but I did pick up a few bucks playing at wedding receptions and funerals.

The accordion followed me to college, and it stayed with me in later life. For a time I was the keyboard in Delbert Keith's "The Collegiates" dance band. I went on to play everything from Rotary Valentine parties to Saturday night parties at the golf course. Up until my debilitating tremor shut me down, I played hymns at Sunday mass.

Roger and his Accordion

As a 7th or 8th grader, I became interested in astronomy. A newspaper ad led me to a Sky Scope, a three-inch reflector telescope for $25, and from that time on many hours were spent in the backyard at night. Saving my dollars eventually led to a Unitron refractor. I felt like Galileo the first time I saw Saturn's rings and Jupiter's moons. My telescope was actually locked up for a month or two following a parent-teacher conference. Too little time was spent hitting the books.

I was, and still am today, an almost compulsive collector. It might have started with baseball cards. It seems that wherever I went, that cigar box with sixteen decks of cards held together with rubber bands was a part of me. Those were the days of the St. Louis Browns, Washington Senators, and Philadelphia Athletics. But it didn't stop at baseball cards.

My introduction to the world of coin collecting came in 1952 when on my 10th birthday Aunt Marion and Uncle Bill gave me a cellophane bag of foreign coins they had purchased at Marshall Fields. Though the foreign coins with their odd shapes were fascinating, it wasn't long before I was filling a Whitman album with Lincoln cents. Today I sometimes wonder what scarce dates I discarded if a space was already filled.

At about this same time I was earning five dollars on Saturdays by scrubbing the rest rooms and offices of the machine shop where my father was a partner. That five dollars turned over numerous times a week as rolls of pennies, nickels, and dimes were exchanged after school at Chicago's Beverly State Bank on Ashland Avenue.

By my 12th birthday, I had complete sets of mercury dimes, buffalo nickels, and Jefferson nickels. My Lincolns lacked a few rare dates I bought at Ben's Stamp & Coin on 31 N. Clark. At this same period in time, a few Barber coins and liberty head nickels could still be found in change.

Lawn mowing and snow shoveling had soon expanded my earning

power, and I became focused on liberty standing quarters. I still see my greatest find ever as a 1924 quarter in XF-AU condition that I spotted in the cash register of a Robert Hall clothing store.

During my college years (1960-1964), and then in the early years of our marriage, my coin collecting went dormant. It reached a low in the early 1970's when I sold my Lincolns and mercury dimes to buy new appliances. However, by the late 1970's, my collecting interest rekindled. The object of my attention was my incomplete set of liberty standing quarters, but with three daughters in school, it would have to wait. Eventually I thought again about the liberty standing quarters, and in early 2016 I decided to go for it. Today the set is complete.

Other than sports, model airplane building, along with the coin collecting, became major pass times in my youth. Twenty-five cent model airplane kits required cutting sticks to a certain length with a razor knife, cutting pre-marked pieces out of balsa sheets with that same razor, and then gluing wings, tail sections, and fuselage together over patterns to assemble a skeleton. Wings, tail, and fuselage were then covered with sheer tissue paper and then stretched by steaming over a water pan on the kitchen stove. It was highly delicate work, and I can't help but wonder if it is a lost art today.

Those rubber band powered model airplanes led to models powered by tiny gas engines. I didn't get into radio-controlled models, and as my models more often than not crash landed, my interest soon faded, and model HO gauge trains took their place with a passion.

My father, and my brother to a lesser degree, also got into the HO trains. J.B. and I had a layout along the east and north walls of our bedroom, and as I built model railroad cars and created scenery, dad built engines and laid track. Like the model airplane engines, the Wheaties license plates, and the coins, I still have our HO gauge trains.

Fishing, followed by hunting, eventually became my most passionate pass-times of all. Cedar Lake, IN introduced my brother and me to fishing, but my father nurtured my insatiable hunger to take both fishing and hunting to greater degrees of adventure.

It began with a boat-building project in our basement during the winter of 1952-1953. I learned about marine plywood and brass screws. That boat, along with my grandfather's venerable Johnson Sea-Horse Three outboard motor with flywheel and detached starter rope, went to Minnesota's Pelican Lake for five days of camping and fishing. We slept in a canvas wall tent, cooked over an open fire, and caught big northern pike and huge crappies that we buried in the sawdust of an old ice house. Pelican Lake laid the groundwork for the next level of camping adventure.

August 1954 found Dad, J.B., and me entering Ontario at International Falls and heading north to Sioux Narrows. At that time, Lake of the Woods was more or less wilderness, and we saw few other fishermen. We caught northern pike, walleyes, and smallmouth bass – the walleyes and smallmouth being new to us.

We returned to the same area the following year, but the conversation around the campfire went like this. "If we carry far more gasoline next year, what do we have with us now that we can do without?" We eliminated the canned goods and pop and trimmed the menu to potatoes, carrots, slab bacon, cooking oil, crackers, flour, eggs, cold cereal, powdered milk, Lipton powdered soup, candy bars, sugar, salt, and pepper. J.B. and I had become proficient with map and compass, and I had confidence in piloting the boat, running the motor, and developing a sixth sense for finding fish. What lay ahead for the summer of 1956?

Dad had learned about Quetico Provincial Park from friends at his work place. These guys were not only sheep hunters, they had taken giant bears on Kodiak. Doing what these guys called adventure thrilled me. Before heading to Quetico in August 1956, Dad acquired a new 12' aluminum boat that J.B. and I could easily carry. We also had a new 7.5 horsepower Scott-Atwater outboard engine.

This time we crossed the Canadian border at Pigeon River and headed for the new highway construction that led to Atikokan. We witnessed chain gangs of men in striped suits breaking up boulders with sledge hammers. We left the car at a ranger fire tower near French Lake where J.B. and I carried the boat to the lake shore. A portage from French to Pickerel Lake put us on near virgin waters. I felt akin to the Voyageurs.

With map and compass we identified every island as we passed. Near treeless islands had been recommended as campsites– few mosquitos, no bears. We caught huge pike, the biggest my forty-seven inch behemoth that went thirty pounds.

The Chicago area held little hunting opportunity, but we did have shirt-tail farm relatives near Manteno, Princeton, and Mendon where we were introduced to cottontails, pheasants, and quail. Again Dad took J.B. and me, and Dad's cousin, Robert Robbins, usually went along. In the far distant future, Dad and Robert would become South Dakotans.

I was in 8th grade and J.B. in 6th when we received Mossberg shotguns for Christmas. We soon acquired the previously mentioned .22's, and it was at Michigan Avenue's Gatley's People Store where J.B. and I acquired our Enfield .303 rifles for $16.88. A formidable handgun was added to my growing collection, and I've been into guns ever since.

I don't know that any youth had a finer journey to adulthood than I.

Perverts and Predators

Chicago, a sprawling city of four million, was paralyzed with fear. On the evening of October 16, 1955, 14 year-old Bobby Peterson, 13 year-old John Schuessler, and 11 year-old Anton Schuessler headed to downtown Chicago to see a movie. Two days later their naked bodies were found in Robinson Woods, a Chicago forest preserve.

On December 28, 1956, the Grimes sisters, 15 year-old Barbara and 13 year-old Patricia, disappeared one evening after heading to a neighborhood movie theatre. As the snow melted, their naked bodies were found on January 22, 1957. Unlike the Peterson-Schuessler murder, the Grimes case remains unsolved. It was a time when the police followed every lead no matter how insignificant.

The date was December 8, 1955. It was a Catholic Church holy day, and there was no school at St. Margaret's. I was a 13 year-old, 6'4" eighth grader, and I was headed downtown to look for some coins for my coin collection. Like Bobby Peterson, the Schuessler brothers, and the Grimes sisters, youths traveling about the city without an adult was a common practice.

For whatever reason, I chose to take the bus that day rather than the Rock Island train. Perhaps cost was a factor. While waiting for a northbound bus at 96th and Halsted Street, a man pulled up in a new Oldsmobile. He wanted to know how to get to Cottage Grove Avenue. I told him to go on to 95th Street and turn right.

He acted confused and asked if I would be willing to show him.

Eventually I yielded to his plea and climbed into the front seat of his car. We made the right turn on 95th. Almost immediately he started asking questions I knew nothing about. Had I ever had my hands in a woman's pants? Had I ever had a blow job? As naïve as I was, I began to get very uncomfortable. I told him to pull over and let me out of the car. He kept on going.

Up came my left leg as I slammed on the brakes. Fear overcame me as I piled out of the car, and I never looked back. I ran home without stopping, flew through the back door, ran up the stairs to my room, threw myself onto my bed, and cried. Mom wanted to know what was wrong. I never regained any composure until dad was at my side, his hand on my shoulder. "What happened?"

Never had I seen such anger in my father, but it wasn't directed at me. He called the police. The front doorbell rang after supper that night. It was two police officers, no doubt detectives, wearing suits. They wanted to take me downtown the following morning to meet with a sketch artist. I told them I had school. Mom and Dad said it would be alright. The drawing looked good, but I was never called upon to pick someone from a lineup. I did a lot of growing up over that incident.

It was during the summer of 1963 that I encountered a life-threatening incident. I was with Mary, a good friend and grade school classmate. We were parked in Burnham Woods of the East Side steel mills neighborhood. I loved my summer job at Republic Steel, and I wanted to show Mary where I worked. A car pulled up behind us, its headlights on high beam. It proceeded to back up a few feet, and then move forward and bump our rear bumper with its front. This went on for a minute or two. I should have pulled out of there! Why I didn't I'll never know.

The driver got out of the car and approached my driver's side window. He had a crowbar in his hand.

"We want the girl!" he ordered.

"No way!" I replied. When he raised his arms to smash in my window, I pulled my Smith & Wesson .357 mag from under the seat and pointed it right at him. Fortunately he made a hasty retreat. So did we.

A Time of Racial Conflict

I cannot talk about my formative years on the south side of Chicago without noting the presence of racial conflict. It was there, and it affected the lives of all.

Going into the sixties, I don't believe there were any African-American homes or families south of 95 Street or west of Halsted with the exception of an old apartment house around 98th and Morgan that had been there before the newer "white" homes had been built. During my college days (1960-1964) my home turf developed into a racial battleground.

Breaking up an all-white neighborhood was known as "block busting." The offensive strategy was simple and effective. Tension was maintained by street gangs such as the Egyptian Cobras patrolling the neighborhood in black cars with a painted, full length cobra on the doors and front fenders. Unscrupulous realtors used the mail, telephone, and knocks on the front door to offer white homeowners many times what their homes were worth. Midnight moves were orchestrated as well as secret relocation. Waking up to a new, African-American next door neighbor was a matter of time.

The location of that first fallen home became a war zone. While payment for that first house was many times its value, the neighboring homes fell like dominos at what would be a fraction of their worth. For white homeowners, their net worth was at stake. Would our neighbors be able to hold on?

City blocks elected block captains, and my father was a block captain. Weekly meetings, often in our living room-dining room area, were faithfully conducted. Does anyone have a new job? Do you need to sell your home and move? Don't panic!

It didn't take long. Across the alley and across 96th Street, the second house from the corner on Peoria Street housed the Lee's, a new black family. The Parkers were gone, never to be seen again so far as I know. On that first early evening I was in front of our garage working under my car. I heard familiar voices coming down the alleyway. As they passed, I saw gas cans and ball bats. The neighborhood homes were of brick, but most garages were made of wood. They were going to burn Lee's garage. Within minutes squad cars stormed the area, but the damage was done. "Who was responsible?" the police asked.

"Dad, I know who did it. Should I tell the police?"

"Your mother, brothers, sister, and I have to live here. You get to go back to South Dakota. Keep it to yourself."

I believe that four years later the Wiltz family was the only white family on the 9600 block of Sangamon Street. Our black neighbors treated us with respect. In fact, I went fishing in the Mississippi River with the guys across the alley. By this time my Mom was confined to a wheel chair with multiple sclerosis. She needed ground level living space, and the family moved to a single-floor ranch style home in Evergreen Park, a western suburb. To my knowledge, dad received fair market value for our Sangamon Street home. The neighborhood remained middle-class.

During the early to mid-sixties, potential conflict loomed on every corner. It was early June 1961. I was home for the summer after spending my first year of college on the campus of South Dakota State College in Brookings, SD. My father, brother, and I were looking over my 1948 Plymouth, a recent fifty-dollar purchase, in front of the garage.

Previous trips to and from Brookings had been on the Chicago & Northwestern "Dakota 400," a train I boarded in Chicago's downtown La Salle Street Station. The route was discontinued during the year, and I was forced to find another means of transportation. The Plymouth had run well during the 630 mile trip, and the five dollars apiece I collected from three Chicago bound passengers paid for the gas.

Tim, a friend from Sangamon Street's 9500 block, had spotted me and ambled over. I hadn't seen him since Christmas. "Let's head down to the Greek's and I'll treat on milkshakes," I offered. Dad and Byron, my brother, declined, but Tim accepted. We headed east down 96th Street toward Halsted. The Greek's, an ice cream shop, lay on the southwest intersection of Halsted and 96th Street. When we hit the alleyway that separates Halsted and Green Streets, we spotted a dozen or so African-American youths in the parking lot.

"I'm not going any further," remarked Tim. "That's nothing but trouble." I should have followed his lead.

"Stay here if you like," I offered, "but I came here for a milkshake, and that's what I'm going to do. I'll be careful. What flavor do you want?"

When I reached for the door handle after walking around the group on the north side of the building, I said, "Excuse me." A blow on the head from behind sent me to the ground, but I was quickly back on my feet, my back against the wall. As the gang surrounded me, a guy of my own height waved a knife back and forth in front of my nose as he muttered, "Let's go a few rounds, white boy."

One of Dad's bits of wisdom came immediately to mind. "If you're ever in a tight spot with your back against the wall, make the first move." I drove my knee into him and swung a forearm across his face. Going over the top of him, I was off and running for the alley and 96th

Street, the gang on my heels. I outran all of them. Spring football had left me in good shape.

By this time two things had apparently happened. The Greek called the police, and Tim went after my father and brother. As I ran up 96th, I saw my father and brother running toward me. One was wielding a crow bar, the other a long-handled axe. As we were about to converge, squad cars flooded the scene, red lights flashing. The gang headed for Halsted Street. Having been away from home since Christmas, I wasn't aware of the degree of racial tension in the neighborhood. It was my own stubborn fault.

In spite of brushes with bodily harm, I never bore animosity toward the black community. I credit my parents. As a child, I asked my parents what the signs "Semi-Private Club" on the fronts of restaurants or at the entrances of golf courses meant. I was told it meant no black people. The injustice troubled me.

Civil Rights was a popular news item. Martin Luther King was marching in nearby Evergreen Park, only two miles west of our house. I probably rode my bike to see the action on 95th street, but I just don't remember for sure. The local news on television that night carried some very vocal and angry black ministers who condemned King for inciting trouble in a time when they felt they were making good progress. At the time, it left me with mixed emotions about King.

I've gone through much of my life with those mixed feelings about Martin Luther King as he was not always the hero he is generally accepted as today. He was said to be a womanizer who was financed by the communist party. During the 70's and into the 80's, we often had FBI agents give presentations at the Wagner High School where I was the principal. They presented King as J. Edgar Hoover's foremost public enemy.

Hero or not, King's targeting Evergreen Park was a well-chosen goal. Evergreen Park had a volunteer fire department. This meant two things. A black family in Evergreen Park would probably have a fire, and most likely, the fire department wouldn't show up.

As King's assets outweigh his liabilities, I accept him as a hero today, but I will never rank him with Jackie Robinson. I see King's status today as the product of a propaganda campaign. I'd guess that Congress created the holiday and the media cultivated it. I realize that this didn't make it wrong.

To young Roger, a more significant thing occurred in our own Oakdale Park. The young Chicago Cub shortstop sensation, Ernie Banks, came to our park. He gave us autographed baseballs, and he took the time to personally show me how to hold a baseball bat. This 8th grade boy had no greater hero. In looking back, it was the first time a lot of us white boys met a black man, who, along with second baseman Gene Baker, were the Cubs' first black ball players. What a positive impression. We'll never know just how far that visit from Banks went. It was very sad that Mr. Cub, Ernie Banks, didn't live to see the 2016 World Series.

Concerning positive progress with the racial injustice that prevailed, I literally felt the positive effects men like Ernie Banks, Gale Sayers, and later Walter Peyton had on my "white" environment. They were heroes.

The Threat of Nuclear Annihilation

The fear of nuclear annihilation was very real. Popular science magazines were full of plans for backyard nuclear fallout shelters. Nikita Khrushchev, General Secretary of the Soviet Union Communist Party, was pounding the heel of his shoe on a podium as he told us, "We will bury you. Your children's children will live under communism."

The threat became all the more eminent when the Soviets put Sputnik I into orbit on October 4, 1957. It told the world that they had a missile capable of launching an intercontinental nuclear warhead. This was foremost in all our minds as we discussed it in first period sophomore geometry class. Our own inability was further reinforced on the evening news when we watched Navy Vanguard missiles blowup on the launching pad in an attempt to launch a two-pound satellite. Up until this time, our Army, Air Force, and Navy competed with each other instead of working together. We would learn quickly as the "Space Race" was launched.

The situation continued to escalate when we positioned Jupiter-C missiles armed with nuclear warheads in Turkey in April of 1962. The Soviets were quick to counter. In August 1962, a U-2 surveillance aircraft provided evidence of missile sites on Cuban soil. Turnabout in the form of the Cuban Missile Crisis was fair play. I often wondered about the cards President Kennedy held when he called the Russian's hand and ordered them to pull their missiles. I found out in the fall of 1971, and even though I am venturing into my life as a South Dakotan, the subject of Book II, now is the time to relate that story.

As high school principal/guidance counselor at Burke, SD in 1971, I was invited by the Air Force to visit the Denver area Lowry Air Force Base as well as the Air Force Academy in Colorado Springs. On our return trip home, a technical glitch forced us to spend an unscheduled day at Rapid City's Ellsworth Air Force base. While at Ellsworth, we inspected a missile silo as well as a manned B-52 bomber.

During a de-briefing session that followed our tour, I asked the general in command if B-52's were more or less obsolete. His answer shocked me. Concerning the Soviet threat during the Cuban Missile Crisis, he told us that according to intelligence, 96% of our B-52's would reach Soviet targets. He added that if only 4% reached target, there would be no more Soviet Union. Numbers mattered.

Summer Employment

From the time I needed change in my pocket for five-cent popsicles or penny candy at Lee's, a neighborhood family convenience store on the northeast corner of 97th and Genoa, I had the money. I don't remember ever asking mom for a nickel or a dime, and we had no allowance. My revenue was generated by shoveling snow, mowing lawns, doing yard work, or collecting pop bottles for the two-cent deposit.

As far back as my memory will serve, perhaps 1947 or 1948, my father worked for L.A. Goodman Manufacturing Company near 63rd and Wentworth. He was a tool and die maker. The Goodman's I remember produced plastic illuminated Santa Clauses and plastic beer advertisements.

In 1954 or thereabouts, Dad left Goodman's and went into partnership with John and Stanley Para to form Para Products, a machine shop near 79th and Western Avenue. At first dad worked long hours including Saturdays. I became a janitor of sorts on Saturdays and received the princely sum of five dollars for cleaning the two offices, the adjoining women's rest room, and the men's restroom in the shop area. The grease caked on the men's room wash basins required more scrubbing than the rest of the job combined.

When machinists were in short supply, they sat me in front of a lathe and taught me to read a micrometer. I was paid a dollar an hour for turning custom screws and bolts. This generally followed later on Saturday after my janitor duties were fulfilled.

My first full-time job came in the summer of 1960 following high school graduation. My Aunt Marion and Uncle Bill worked for the Belt Railroad, and their influence landed me a job with Wabash Fibre Boxes. After a day or two of unloading heavy rolls of paper from railroad boxcars, a dangerous job, I was switched to the shipping dock to load semi-trailers. I soon realized the change related to being literate. Many of my co-workers, primarily southerners, printed their numbers and letters backwards.

Finished folded boxes were in bundles of 25 or 50. When we were to load 500 size 109 Curtis Candy boxes, someone had to figure out how many bundles to put in the trailer. The guys would look at me. When I told them to load ten bundles without using pencil or paper, they would point me out to other workers and whisper in amazement. To them I was a human calculator. In spite of my "mathematical genius," we all got along quite well. A great sign hung on the wall by the foreman's office. WASTE IS CAUSING WABASH MONEY. YOU ARE WABASH! At Wabash we were non-union.

Between my summer Wabash job and room and board financial aid at South Dakota State, I had enough money to cover my freshman year of college with a few dollars to spare.

During the summers of 1961 and 1962, I worked for Galassi Cut Stone in Worth, IL. The stone yard was at 106th and Southwest Highway and I drove to work every day in the 1948 Plymouth I bought for $50 in South Dakota at the end of my freshman year.

Vic Galassi, owner and operator of Galassi Cut Stone, married my father's first cousin, Irene Robbins. I learned of the truck driving job through the family grapevine, and delivering limestone window and door sills to building sites paid better than Wabash. Vic Galassi was short-tempered and not easy to work for, and when he hired me he said he had fired other relatives and that he would fire me.

Limestone sills had natural faults, and it was inevitable that one would crack sooner or later during delivery. When it first happened to me, Vic had a screaming fit and threatened to fire me. When I replied that he would have already fired me if I wasn't making money for him, he smiled. I liked my job and enjoyed working outside and learning more about the south and west suburbs. I also learned some Spanish and a little about Puerto Rico through my co-workers. Vic once lectured me about becoming too close to them, but they were my friends.

My brother, John Byron, graduated from Mendel in 1962 where he was a stellar athlete in wrestling and track. A city shotput champion and better athlete than I ever dreamed of being, he would also attend South Dakota State. When I headed for Galassi Cut Stone in the morning, J.B. took a CTA bus to Sherwin-Williams. More often than not, he had to scrub paint from the pores of his skin when he got home from work.

In the summer of 1963, jobs were not easy to find. My closest friend, Don Kilgallon, had a summer job at Republic Steel in South Chicago. Don lived in the mills area, and his father had been a steel man all his life. Don suggested that J.B. and I apply at Republic.

Both J.B. and I stood 6'5" and weighed 210 pounds. Our bodies held nary an ounce of fat. As we stood in line that morning in front of the Republic Steel employment office, a man approached us with some questions.

"Can you guys work in 125 degrees heat?"

"No problem," we replied. He's exaggerating we said to ourselves.

"Can you handle 1500 pound loads of manganese in a wheelbarrow?"

"No problem," we again replied. A wheelbarrow can't hold 1500 pounds of manganese we thought to ourselves.

"Follow me!" the man said.

We were soon seated in compartmental booths of the employment office. We filled out applications, took some aptitude tests, put pegs in holes and washers on bolts, and finished the battery with a personal interview and a physical. For the next couple of days we were saturated with safety instructions. Come to work alert, well-rested, and sober! Men could and did die in the mill. Republic Steel was a defining milestone in my life. I learned about unions, timeclocks, and management, and I learned some valuable life lessons.

When we walked through the tunnel on that first day of work, I wondered if I would walk out. We were told that as long as we felt that way and respected the potential danger, we would do just fine. My car's windshield now had a decal on it. "I Make Steel!" I was very proud of that.

As the furnaces could only be shutdown at prohibitive expense, the mill ran 24 hours a day 7 days a week. Most employees, myself and brother included, worked a swing shift. The shifts ran 7:00 a.m. to 3:00 p.m., 3:00 p.m. to 11:00 p.m., and 11:00 p.m. to 7:00 a.m. We worked five consecutive days, took off two, and returned on the shift that followed our last shift. For example, if I worked the 7 to 3, I returned to the 3 to 11. Most of the guys liked the 3 to 11 shift best. We called the 11 to 7 the "graveyard shift." There was no lunch time. Lunch was eaten "on the fly."

Our first 30 days on the job was a probationary period. Once our 30 days were in, union dues were taken from our paycheck. Toward the end of the 30 days, foremen would ask us if we had our 30 days in before asking us to do something that might be dangerous. If we were union, we might go to our union grievance rep and report our foreman for asking us to perform an unsafe practice. Management was non-union.

Once we were union (United Steel Workers), we could say "show me how" if we felt an order was unsafe. When I was working the stripper crane where red hot ingots were pulled from the molds, the foreman asked me to paint some numbers on ingots that were still radiating intense heat. I was union and I told him to show me how. He backed off immediately.

During the summer of '63, I made more than enough money at Republic to pay for school and have ample spending money in my pocket. Other than hourly wages that ran $2.00-$3.00 per hour, there was much overtime. Overtime paid time-and-a-half, and we received overtime anytime we didn't have a 16 hour break between shifts.

For example, if the foreman asked me at the end of a shift if I wanted to work the following shift, I received overtime for the next shift. Then, because I didn't have a 16 hour break before the next day's shift, I received overtime for that coming shift. If we caught a holiday such as the 4th of July or Labor Day, we received two-and-a-quarter times regular pay. If we came into the holiday on overtime, we received time-and-a-half times double-and-a-quarter.

I began my Republic steel mill career in Mold Prep. When empty upright cast iron molds rolled in from the stripper crane on special railroad flat cars, we vacuumed them out, "sugared" the insides with a black sugary powder, and mounted new "hot tops" on the molds. We first relined the hot tops with a special brick. I soon became proficient with a trowel in my hand. I would roughly estimate the molds at 40 X 40 inches in diameter and 10-12 feet high.

If the steel going into a set of molds was an "aircraft" heat, a government inspector often inspected our mold jobs for cleanliness. Aircraft jobs had a zero tolerance for dirty steel.

Seven workers were on a Mold Prep crew. Three could get the job done, and the four "extras" often sat around and talked about how the company was exploiting us. The veteran crews were more than willing to let the summer college boys do the work. At about this same time the union negotiated 13 week paid vacations for veteran employees, and summers found many college boys at work filling vacation spots.

I wondered how such a system could work at a profit. It didn't. The Chicago plant closed down in the 70's because cheaper steel could be manufactured in Japan or China. Greed was killing American industry. It was also slowly killing middle class America.

I was the only white boy on our seven man crew. We became good friends, and I'll never forget the day they wanted to give me a ride home. They were giggling to themselves as they thought about a carload of black guys dropping me off in a white neighborhood.

"Wiltz, where did you say you lived?" asked Lonnie.

"9601 Sangamon. That's three blocks west of Halsted," I answered. The guys looked at each other.

"Can't be. Brothers live there," countered Carter.

"Not in my house! We're the last of the white folks." They took it in stride.

Carter was the elder on our crew, and I'd guess he was pushing 65. He came to work every day dressed in suit, white shirt, and tie, and he carried a leather brief case. Off came the suit and on went the coveralls in the locker room. His neighbors saw him as an executive.

Being 3rd Helper on an electric furnace was my brother' first assignment. It paid slightly more than Mold Prep, and he learned immediately that the bit about heat and 1500 pounds in a wheelbarrow wasn't just talk. Hitting a small door opening on the side of an electric furnace with a tightly packed shovel full of ore required a skilled flick of the wrists in intolerable radiant heat. One learned to hit that opening from further distances as skill progressed. Over the next two summers, I also spent time as 3rd Helper.

Frank Todd, aka "The Man," was the plant superintendent. He stood tall in his white shirt, tie, and hardhat, and he was god-like to every employee in the mill. I was on 3rd Helper duty one day when an electrode slipped deeper into a furnace. Someone had to go onto the top of the furnace and wrap a chain from the crane around the fallen electrode. No one, myself included, would do it. Along came "The Man." He climbed the ladder with authority and wrapped the chain. The legend grew. I would later have a second encounter with Mr. Todd.

The most miserable mill job I ever had was cleaning the flues under an open hearth furnace. I worked with a partner, and it was on again, off again, every ten minutes. The temperature in those flues was 130 degrees.

I came out of the flues and looked out over the switchyard. "Fred, Look at the beach! Look at all those girls!" Fred called the foreman. The foreman called a plant physician who shined a flashlight into my eyes. They took me home. I was hallucinating, and I had the remainder of the day off with pay.

During the summer of '64, I was a 2nd Ladle Man. I was in Republic Steel's "Mission Control," and the enormity of everything around me – the monster furnaces across the molten slag pit, the mammoth ladles, the behemoth crane – filled me a sense of self-importance that made me feel like I mattered on a world stage.

The 1st Ladle Man raised or lowered the stopper in the bottom of the ladle that controlled the flow of molten steel into the molds that were lined up along our gangway. He held a box with "open" and "close" buttons. The crane operator (some of them were women) moved the ladle from mold to mold as they were filled with orange-white molten steel that gurgled and splashed like water. In spite of the thick woolen full-length coats we wore, droplets of hot steel would sometimes fall between our necks and collar and roll down our backs.

As 2nd Ladle Man, my primary job was taking samples. I first lined-up sample molds the size of half-gallon milk cartons in front of the molds. I was given a set of steel strips with numbers on them, and I folded a strip over the side of a sample mold so that the numbers were on the outside. As a large mold was being filled, I asked the 1st Ladle Man to stop the flow. With a very long-handled ladle that looked like a giant soup ladle, I put the ladle under the location of the flow and asked the 1st Ladle Man to give me a shot. I then pulled my ladle from the flow and poured my sample into my numbered mold. Someone from the lab would later pick up the samples. Holding that "soup ladle" under the flow required a great deal of strength.

As a ladle empties, it reaches a point where only molten slag remains in the ladle as slag floats. The difference in color between molten steel and molten slag is slight, and it took a week before I could see the color change and call for the end of the pour. Once I recognized it, I wondered how I didn't see it from the start.

As 2nd Ladle Man, I sometimes had a second far more dangerous job when we poured a lead heat. Lead cannot be alloyed with steel in the furnace because all the lead would go off as a vapor. To alloy steel with lead, lead pellets had to be added to the flow of molten steel as it was poured into the molds. I held a heavy canvas hose right at the nozzle that put out a steady stream of lead pellets that were identical to shotgun pellets. I was to shoot a stream of lead pellets directly into the molten steel flow.

A large system of overhead ductwork sucked in the orange vapor produced when the lead pellets met the molten steel. If and when we noted that the orange fumes weren't being sucked into the vacuum system, we were to drop what we were doing and clear out! Inhaling a breath of orange fume meant certain lead poison death.

And so it happened. I knew what lead was worth, and rather than seeing thousands of dollars worth of lead go to the slag pit, I held my breath, bent the hose, shut off the air, and then cleared out. I saw myself as a hero, and I expected some sort of commendation.

I was sent to see Mr. Todd. Did he ever cut me down to size! I was thoroughly humiliated, received three days off without pay, and returned as a laborer to clean open hearth flues. I needed that, and from that point on I saw it as a life-defining experience.

At that point I had my B.S. Degree, Betsy and I had serious intentions, and I planned to return to SDSC and do graduate work while waiting for Betsy to finish school. At the end of the summer, Republic Steel called me into the personnel office and offered me a 13 month trainee position that paid thirteen thousand dollars – big money in 1964. When I told them that my degree wasn't in metallurgy, they told me it was their decision, not mine. My being a steel man was put to rest when Betsy let me know she didn't want to live in South Chicago. It was the right call.

One last steel mill story. I was working the graveyard shift in mold prep when the crew sent me to the canteen for bacon & egg sandwiches. Some guy in the canteen asked me if I would circulate his union campaign posters in Mold Prep, and he offered me two tickets for the United Steel Workers "Fun Day" for doing it. I agreed. As it happened, my best friend, Don Kilgallon, and I were both free for the union "Fun Day." We headed for the Lincolnshire Country Club.

We arrived around 9:00 a.m., and I hadn't had breakfast. Some "fat cat" union boss spotted me and signaled for me to come over to his table.

"Where do you work?" he asked.

"Mold prep," I answered. We had talked for a few minutes when he suggested some breakfast. He signaled for Trixie, the waitress, to come to our table. Trixie's waitress outfit was noticeably revealing.

"What would you like?" asked Trixie.

"What can I have?" I responded.

"You name it!" countered Trixie.

"How about a four-egg omelet with ham, bacon, cheese, green

peppers, and onions, a large orange juice, and an apple turnover?" I quipped with a grin on my face. Of course they couldn't do it, or so I thought. I would soon learn that Trixie meant her "you name it" line. I should have asked for steak.

My union brother made small talk as I consumed a delightful omelet, and he eventually got around to asking how I liked Trixie.

"Trixie's just fine.....maybe a little older than me.....but really put together," I replied a wee bit uncomfortably.

"How would you like to go upstairs with Trix?" questioned my little union buddy. I anticipated the offer, and I was halfway afraid. I looked over at Don and suggested that we play some golf. We spent the day riding around the course in a cart. We were half blitzed by noon, and we spent the afternoon sobering up.

I can't prove that Trixie was a hooker, but I don't think the offer to go upstairs with Trix involved a Scrabble game. The United Steel Workers had certainly spent some money on their "Fun Day."

A Skeleton in our Closet

At this point in my life's story, one might get the impression that I experienced a wonderful stress-free youth other than the Soviet threat, racial conflict, and a few sexual predators. This wasn't quite the case as alcoholism touched our lives.

My Grandma Olson enjoyed a quart or two of beer before bedtime. To her credit, I never saw her under the influence during the day, but I don't know how she would have functioned without it. Her two children, my mother and my Uncle Roger, were alcoholics. My mother would go for months without a drink, but then I would come home from school and find her passed out on the kitchen floor. As a little kid, I didn't understand the nature of the problem until it was explained to me at an age where I might comprehend.

It would pass, and life as usual would return the following day. It created a situation where I was afraid to bring friends home from school for fear of what we might find. In later years after my mother's passing, I asked Dad about it. Mom neither drank in her teens nor the early years of their marriage. It began after the birth of my brother John Byron. Were J.B.'s and my normal sibling confrontations stressful obstacles? While I'll never know the cause, I do realize that alcoholism is an illness.

My Uncle Roger, a WWII naval officer, was a great guy who has left me with fond memories. We never saw them very often as they first lived in Riverside, CA and then Newport News, VA. I did know that my uncle had an alcohol problem, and to his credit, he spent the later years of his life as a reformed AA member. Aunt Frankie and Uncle Ole are gone. Uncle Roger's youngest daughter, Becky, recently succumbed to cancer. Nancy, now my only first cousin, and I remain in touch.

My younger brother, John Byron, never drank any more in college than the rest of us guys. I never realized that he might have a problem until he came to our South Dakota home to pheasant hunt in later years. After supper he wanted me to go with him to a local bar. I couldn't as I was a high school principal with school the next day. He preferred a bar to our visiting, and it was very late when he returned that night.

John Byron Wiltz would take his own life. Our family doctor tells me it was alcohol related, and I'll talk more about it in a later chapter. Oh how I miss that guy. We had so many plans for our retirement.

Book II South Dakota

My life as a South Side Chicagoan made a four-year transition through my college years, 1960-1964, to that of being a South Dakotan. I legally became a South Dakotan in the fall of 1960 when the purchase of a resident hunting license necessitated the acquisition of a South Dakota driver's license even though I didn't have a vehicle until the spring of 1961. Residency enabled me to pay resident tuition. Summers and summer employment remained in Chicago through the summer of 1964.

Through my five working summers (1960, 1961, 1962, 1963, 1964) the buying power of those Chicago earned dollars came to astonish me. I made almost as much money in three summer months of Chicago steel mill as I made in my first nine months of teaching in South Dakota, and the teaching required a college degree!

The College Years 1960-1964

D ad took me to the downtown LaSalle Street Station in early September of 1960 where I boarded the Chicago & Northwestern "Dakota 400." That train more or less followed Highway 14 from Chicago to Rapid City, South Dakota. The stop I most remember was Rochester, MN where the train all but emptied with Mayo Clinic customers. From Rochester on, it was the porters and I.

The loneliest moment of my life occurred as that train rolled out of the station. Up to that point I had never been away from family, and I was hurting. Dad had wished me luck, but he had also reminded me of his expectations. He wanted me to be an engineer, and I registered in civil engineering. I had no idea what I wanted to be, and I had thought that GR or General Registration would have been more appropriate.

Based on my gear - a trunk, golf clubs, and my recently purchased Winchester Model 97 shotgun, one might have thought I was going on vacation. As it turned out, my 1st quarter grades looked like I was on vacation.

It was around midnight and every bit as dark as midnight when the train stopped at the Brookings, SD station. I was the only one to disembark. Three shadowy figures, all dressed in trench coats, approached. "Are you Wiltz?" the tall guy asked. I would soon learn that I could not have been met by nicer guys – John Sterner, Mike Sterner, and Ron Frank. They took me to my new home, Gym Dorm, where John and Mike lived.

73

Freshman Orientation was a busy affair. We were tested in math, chemistry, and English grammar. We were also given the MMPI or Minnesota Multiphasic Personality Inventory. "Was I a messenger sent from God?" I colored in the squares as quickly as I could, but they were on to me as they made me take it over again.

We also met as a large group in the Administration Building Theatre where they told us that the persons on either side of us would be gone by the end of the year. The freshman chemistry requirement would be a primary cause. Not very hospitable. I would years later ask my good friend, Curt Kaberna, if he remembered that day. He did, and he went home. Curt would have been a great engineer.

In the fall of 1960, South Dakota State College tuition for a fulltime student was the same whether one took 12 or 20 hours, and because I had been taught to be a "get the most for your money guy," I carried as many hours as I could work into my schedule. For me, graduating in four years was not a problem semester hour wise. Grade Point Average was a problem, and it took a senior year rally to get my GPA up to the minimum requirement. I'm not proud of that.

Freshman Year 1960-1961

I didn't know it when I moved in, but 1960-1961 was Gym Dorm's final year. It would be fair to call the place infamous. To say the least there was minimal supervision, and our coaches rarely made an appearance. I know of only one occasion where this happened. Roommate Jerry Ochs and I had been skipping chemistry lab to go pheasant hunting, and our coach, Ralph Ginn, had unbeknownst to us come down and confiscated our shotguns. They were later returned on the promise that there would be no more class skipping. Other than Jerry, who was from Aberdeen, my Gym Dorm roommates were Marvin Fluth of Bridgewater, SD, and Dave Westbrock of Brown's Valley, MN.

Two years of ROTC (Reserve Officers Training Corps) was required of all males for graduation, and I chose Army ROTC over Air Force ROTC as it gave me the opportunity to become familiar with an M1 Garand rifle. We were encouraged to make use of the rifle range in the armory basement, and I took advantage of the opportunity. It was discovered that I could flat out shoot, and they wanted me on the rifle team. I declined as I thought I was busy enough with football. This was a very bad decision. Rifle team might have saved me from some major problems down the line.

As a freshman, I also spent time in the wrestling room under the watchful eye of Coach Warren Williamson, who also served as our "Bunny Team" freshman football coach. Guys like John and Mike Sterner, Ron Frank, and Frank Kurtenbach tossed me around with ease, my heart wasn't in it, and I quit wrestling after my freshman year.

It would prove to be a huge mistake as wrestling would one day become a huge part of my life. Today I sorely regret walking out of that wrestling room.

When I told Coach Williamson that I was quitting, I felt like his eyes literally burned through me. He asked if the Chicago Fire had gone out, or whether it was still smoldering. I found it difficult to face him after that.

Some years later he sent me a hand-written letter on stationary depicting the new SDSU Frost Arena. He congratulated me on my coaching success, and that priceless letter "lifted" a huge guilt rock from my shoulders.

Engineering chemistry and algebra was a challenge I barely survived, and I had no desire to be an engineer. I switched my major to art in the spring without worrying about what my father would say. I had always enjoyed drawing, and I'm certain I was influenced by the on campus Harvey Dunn collection. I immediately enrolled in a design and a drawing & composition class. What I would do with an art major I had no idea.

As the spring quarter progressed, I realized that in spite of my doing well in the art courses, majoring in art wasn't my thing. Perhaps college wasn't my thing. At this same time my English Composition instructor had assigned a research paper. He gave us a choice of topics, and at the same time discouraged us from choosing "A Psycho-Freudian Interpretation of Hamlet" as he didn't believe any of us were capable of handling it. In so doing, he must have triggered a challenge that inspired me to delve into Hamlet's relationship with his ghost father. Mr. Morgan approached me one day as I was leaving class.

"Mr. Wiltz, you're quite perceptive. Did you know you can write?"

"I had no idea I could do much of anything," I countered.

"I have a favor to ask. In your paper you get into the Oedipus complex and Hamlet's relationship with his father. May I borrow your thoughts for my doctoral dissertation if I give you full credit?"

"Use anything you like," I answered. "Mr. Morgan, you mentioned my writing ability. In your estimation, might I be an English Major?" His positive feedback had my wheels turning. There was hope. It has always amazed me how a seemingly insignificant happening can change the course of personal history.

During that spring quarter I also took typing over the noon hour. This would prove to be a great move as an English major would require extensive writing. It was a time when students often paid to have someone type compositions for them. This was big business in the girls' dorms.

It was during Thanksgiving week that a fellow student in one of my classes asked me if I was going back to Chicago for the Thanksgiving break. As I wasn't, he invited me to a little party he was hosting on Friday night. I welcomed the invitation as I was already thinking about the empty dorm. None of the guys had thought about what I would be doing, and I wasn't going to invite myself.

I was out of my comfort zone from the start. It seemed obvious that the party had been going for a while as cigarette smoke clouded the upstairs apartment. A few bottles of hard liquor seemed to be the extent of the refreshments, and for whatever reason, the girls in the living room weren't all that attractive to me.…..probably because everyone was older than I.

I was thinking about leaving when one of the guys opened a door in the hall from the inside and invited me in. A girl, passed out cold, lay naked on the bed. Four or five guys looked at me.

"You want some of this?" someone asked. I was totally blindsided! I couldn't imagine anyone acting like this. What kind of animals were these guys? I wanted out.

"Are you guys nuts? Wouldn't this be rape? Don't touch her!" I ordered, mostly out of fear, a little bit out of anger.

"You're going to stop us? What are you going to do about it?" snickered another guy. Anger somehow took hold of me.

My words, the look in my eyes, must have somehow sunk in. I went into the front room and ordered the girls to get in the bedroom and get their friend dressed. Get her to the hospital if necessary. I had never before taken charge of any situation with such authority.

It all ended that quickly, and that guy in my class never spoke another word to me. I once read a story that said a boy becomes a man when a man is needed. Maybe I grew up a little bit that night.

Other than freshman football, wrestling, and making new friends, hunting and going home with friends on weekends was the highpoint of my year. One particular visit brings a smile to my face.

I had gone home on a January weekend with Don Huls of Salem, SD. What an experience! What a fantastic family! A stove in the kitchen heated the entire farmhouse, it was below freezing in the upstairs bedroom, and there was frost on the outhouse toilet seat!

The Huls family was up early Saturday morning to milk the cows. That I understood. What surprised me was milking the cows on Sunday morning! When I asked Don's dad, Joe, why he milked cows on Sunday, I thought he was going to rupture something laughing. After mass that morning, Joe and I stood on the front steps of St. Mary's church. As friends passed, he stopped them to say, "This is Wiltz from Chicago. He asked why we milked our cows on Sunday!" Uproarious laughter followed.

Spring football went well enough to make the squad, and I was adjusting to college life even though the Chicago-South Dakota transition was a dose of culture shock. The Chicago & Northwestern had dropped the "Dakota 400" service beyond Rochester, and I was thinking bus for transportation back to Chicago when Jim Redmond of Flandreau, SD was desperate to sell his fine running 1948 Plymouth four-door sedan for fifty dollars. I had my ride home, and I picked up some extra passengers for five dollars a head that paid for gas at 29 cents a gallon.

Sophomore Year 1961-1962

During registration for fall '61 classes I changed my major to English. I also made a very serious mistake of far-reaching consequences that I am still ashamed of today. While I have always been patriotic and very respectful of our flag, I didn't care for ROTC, and there had been rumors floating around campus that in the near future, ROTC would no longer be mandatory. I had to register for ROTC, but no one made me go. The only failing grades I've ever received were for second year ROTC. Toward the end of the school year, I was notified that if I intended to return to SDSC the next fall, I would successfully serve my second year ROTC requirement. I planned to comply.

I was a member of the Jack Rabbit football team that won the North Central Conference title. On Parent's Day we played the North Dakota State Bison. This was before the days of NDSU football dominance, and I, like all team members, played in the game. It was special for me as both Mom and Dad made it to Brookings for the weekend. By this time, Mom was confined to a wheel chair with MS or multiple sclerosis.

I'm a center on the Jackrabbit football team

Today I occasionally think about our football practices and wonder if they relate to any of my neurological problems including my tremor or my peripheral neuropathy. We had a drill called "the meat grinder" where we tried to knock each other unconscious with a forearm shiver. One guy in particular, Dan Cunningham, was positively lethal. In those days, being knocked cold, literally a concussion, was no big deal. It certainly is today.

An incident in the fall of '61 put me on the brink of quitting school. At the time I was renting an upstairs bedroom at 504 Medary from Tex Lewis, an Ag Department faculty member.

As an English Major, a minor in foreign language was required. My German I class was in the Old Engineering building, and Hilda Hasslinger, an excellent teacher, was my instructor.

While class was in progress, three uniformed officers including a campus policeman, a city policeman, and a federal agent burst into the classroom without knocking and asked for Roger Wiltz. When I acknowledged, they grabbed me by the arms and hauled me from the room in front of my peers! I would have gone peacefully had they asked in a civil manner. To his credit, the federal agent advised his partners to back off. They took me to a room in the Brookings city hall for interrogation.

Someone in Brookings was on a bad check writing spree, and a store clerk thought the culprit was tall and wore a ring with a blue stone in it. I was tall, and my Mendel graduation ring had a blue stone. The two locals were gruff, and again the federal agent told them to cool it. One of the officers handed me a book of universal check blanks and told me to write a ten-dollar check on the Ipswich State Bank.

"How do you spell Ipswich?" I asked.

"The same way you did on the check you wrote!" snapped the city officer sarcastically. The interrogation continued.

"What's a pistol doing in your dresser drawer?" asked the city policeman. They had apparently been in my room. Did they have a search warrant? Not to my knowledge.

"I have every right to have a pistol, and what were you doing in my room!" I answered angrily.

There was never an apology, and I came very close to going back to Chicago. Sadly, I would never again have any respect for the campus or Brookings city police. In 1961, student rights on the SDSC campus had a long way to go.

Starting in the fall of '61, and continuing for the next few years, some Chicago guys, primarily but not necessarily from Mendel, came to South Dakota State. It probably had something to do with me in a small way, but I had nothing to do with recruiting. Football players Dennis Dee and Pat Durkin were both Mendel men. So was Mike Sheahan who would go on to become sheriff of Chicago's Cook County.

During the '61-'62 school year, I went on occasional dates, and one stands out in particular. It was a winter Saturday night. All of us were SDSC students, and we had decided to check out the dance in Lake Benton, Minnesota, an 18 mile drive east on Highway 14. Ken, Lois, Phil, and Cass were in the backseat of my 1948 Plymouth, and I was at the wheel with Helaine at my side.

As we approached the town, we could see the sprawling lake off to the northeast. The lake was heavily punctuated with the vehicles, huts, and lanterns of ice fishermen. I had never before experienced ice fishing in any form, and I was excited. "We're early!" I exclaimed. "Let's drive out onto the lake and see how these fishermen are doing." No one objected, and we were soon driving among the many cars and pickup trucks. The anglers were more than willing to visit and show us their fish.

As we approached the northeast end of the fishing encampment, we saw nothing but ice in front of us. No vehicles, no shanties. "Let's drive around for a while before we head to the dance hall," I suggested. Again, no one objected.

It wasn't long before we were attempting to see how fast we could go on this wide open field of ice. As I recall, 85 mph was top end. I soon discovered a thrilling sensation. If I cut the steering wheel hard when going full speed, the car would slowly turn sideways and then go into a wild spin! For the next two hours we were having the time of our lives. Heck with the dance!

We were speeding sideways, out of control, when we suddenly approached a formidable snow drift. When we struck the drift sideways, the ramp-like drift launched us into the air! I don't know how long we were airborne, but when we came down we landed on the roof. I never lost consciousness, but when we landed, I landed on top of little Helaine. She appeared to be lifeless. For a long moment, I feared everyone was dead.

I had just rolled off of Helaine when I heard giggling from the back seat. Helaine came back to life, and we soon discovered that everyone was unscathed. The upside down car doors opened, and the six of us were soon standing alongside the car. We unsuccessfully tried to roll the car back onto its wheels, but it wouldn't budge.

Decision time. Ken would stay with the girls, and Phil and I would go for help. The lights of Lake Benton lay in the distant southwest. We later learned that we made a six mile hike back to town. Before we left, we noted that gas was running onto the ice. We suspected that the motor oil might suffer the same fate. We wisely decided to go to the police station, and before we headed back onto the lake with the chief and two deputies, we obtained some gas and oil from a filling station. As I recall, the police officers thought this was high adventure.

As we returned to the car, the chief asked me if I had any idea of how lucky we were. My stomach turned when he told me there was open water on the lake. How we missed it was an act of God. How close had I come to killing five friends?

With all the man power, we flipped the car back onto its wheels. I then lay on the back seat and kicked the indented roof back into its normal shape. We put gas in the tank, added oil to the engine, and were pleased to discover that the Plymouth started right up.

We feared that the girls might be expelled for missing the dorm curfew, but Miss Birgee, the dorm mother, accepted my explanation. We had been very lucky.

Junior Year 1962-1963

Third Floor South of East Men's Hall was now my residence. My brother, John Byron, lived just down the hall. Tom Larson from Hudson, SD was my roommate, and we hit it off from the start.

Once again I was a member of the Jack Rabbit football team. I no longer had any sort of athletic scholarship, but through the athletic department's influence, I had a free East Men's dorm room as I was an RA or Resident Assistant.

My relationship with the dorm manager started very poorly through no fault of mine. During the first week of classes, someone's room had been broken into. The dorm manager stormed into my room and shouted, "Alright Mr. Chicago, where have you been for the past hour?" I quickly learned to intensely dislike that man. There's no point in mentioning his name, but our trails would cross a few years later when I was keyboard with The Collegiates dance band and he played a sax. We never spoke.

The dorm thing got worse and I was fired from my RA job for the wrong reasons in my opinion. The East Men's RA staff had a meeting with the state fire marshal. We were told that our old wooden dorm with its oil-soaked floors could be a fiery inferno in ninety seconds, and we were to think about evacuation procedures. I did.

I called for a 3rd Floor South meeting and told the guys what the fire marshal had said. I then instructed every resident to have a chair by their window that could be used to break out the window in an emergency. Every room had a radiator beneath the window, and I wanted every resident to have a long enough rope tied to the radiator that could be thrown out and used for evacuation. The plan wasn't perfect, but it was an option.

One of my boys told his parents about the dorm fire hazard, and the parents expressed their concern to the administration. Someone's head had to roll, and it was mine. Though I was fired, I stayed on at East Men's as I liked the guys. East Men's was leveled shortly thereafter.

Dale and Vi Thomas' State Grill was just down Medary Ave. from East Men's, and I was a chef. For guys, The State Grill with its long counter and swivel stools was "the place" to eat. A menu wasn't necessary. It was a hamburger steak with a mountain of fries.

Once football season was over, I came in around 4:00 p.m. I began by dumping about thirty pounds of potatoes into the peeler. I then turned on the deep fryer and heated up the oil. I followed this by cutting the taters into fries with a French fry cutter. Once the oil was hot, I blanched the fries in preparation for rush hour. In the meantime I fired up the grill, made hamburger steak patties from two-and-a-half scoops of hamburger with an ice cream scoop, blanched them on the grill, and then stacked them on the back of the grill. "Heavy on the fries!" was a common command. The job only paid sixty cents an hour, but I fed myself well, and Dale and Vi were like second parents.

I also worked at May's Café across the street from The State Grill. My breakfasts specialized in scrambled eggs. The first two eggs cost a quarter, and each additional egg was five cents. That's a half-dozen scrambled eggs for forty-five cents…..a pretty good breakfast (toast included) for a pretty good price. I was driven to keep busy. I wish more of that energy had gone to course work.

As mentioned, I was on the SDSC football team in the fall of '62. Either we had an open date, or I didn't make the traveling squad that weekend. It's remarkable how one little course of events can bring about a monumental course of events – namely, meeting my future wife.

It was a Friday evening in the fall. Tom, my roommate, and I were walking back to the South Dakota State College campus after an evening of snooker and a few beers at Gussy's. It was 11:30, and we knew we could catch the last half hour of the record hop in the student association ballroom. Perhaps there were some freshmen girls we hadn't "checked over" yet.

We spotted two girls sitting together in a dimly lit corner. The blond had a cast on her arm, and I walked up to her.

"Would you like to dance?"

"I have a cast on my arm."

"I didn't ask you to dance on your hands. What's your name?"

"Betsy," she replied.

Rather than dance, the four of us went down to the cafeteria for donuts and coffee. Tom and I had permission to pheasant hunt on some land south and west of town the next day, and this was foremost on our minds. As this hunting entered the conversation, Ladene, the other girl, mentioned how much she enjoyed pheasant hunting. Like boys, girls are capable of telling a guy anything he wants to hear. As it turned out, Ladene didn't know a shotgun from a blow dryer.

We walked the girls back to Wecota Hall, their dorm. The dorm mother was already flashing the lights on and off, a signal that said it was time to "break-up." It was difficult to talk to a girl about hunting when the couples around you are engaged in heavy breathing. Anyway, Tom and I invited the girls to go hunting with us the next day. They accepted.

When we picked up the girls the next day, I was mildly concerned about their attire. It looked to me like they were dressed for a picnic. It was hardly the right attire for sloughs, corn rows, and sand burrs. I had had visions of the girls carrying our birds if they didn't carry guns, and I would have hated to see Betsy get pheasant blood on that nice blue and white outfit. As it turned out, neither of the girls owned a shotgun although I was impressed with Betsy. She knew that her father used a Model 12 Winchester.

We devised a great plan for this hunt. Tom and I would walk about twenty corn rows apart while the girls zig-zagged between us. The girls were incredulous when we led them to their positions. I don't know what their plans for the day included, but for sure it had nothing to do with zig-zagging through cornfields.

Tom and I, in an attempt to be thoughtful and considerate, compromised. We hunted with the girls until about three o'clock, and then suggested that they rest in the car until we had our limits. Betsy and Ladene were good sports. Their arms and legs were pretty well scratched up from the corn leaves, but there were no complaints. I had to admire them.

There was a slightly romantic side to the trip back to Brookings. Ladene jumped into the backseat while Betsy climbed into the front of my 1948 Plymouth. The front would have been very crowded with Tom, Betsy, and me in the front, so Tom joined Ladene in back. Please don't deduce that the girls were being forward, but they did instigate the change. On the trip out, both girls had been in the back.

The hunt had a happy ending. It was supper time, and we stopped at the Pheasant Café on the south edge of Brookings. For fifty cents, the

Pheasant would cook your pheasant and add salad, French fries, and a Coke. The girls were happy.

Whoever said the years "Twix, Twelve, & Twenty" were troubled times, certainly had it right about "twenty." I went from one bump in the road to the next.

I had met Betsy at a student union record hop, and we went on occasional dates up until the time I invited her to the winter ROTC Military Ball. Though I was fulfilling my ROTC obligation, it was with reluctance as I was becoming increasingly critical of the ROTC program. The Vietnam conflict was heating up, and it seemed to me that recruitment for advanced placement was about quantity, not quality. The word was that if one failed the placement exam, he could repeatedly retake the exam until it was passed. It appeared to me that the bar was being lowered.

I was of a protest mindset that precipitated the biggest mistake of my life – a mistake I regret to this very day. Betsy gave me a boutonniere. While I knew that one didn't put a boutonniere on a military uniform, I rationalized by convincing myself that I wasn't going to insult her. I further desecrated the uniform by placing a few high school track medals on it. On Monday I received notice of my expulsion hearing. I acknowledged that I would be in attendance and argue my case.

We met in the Administration Building. President Hilton Briggs, Colonel Adams, Captain Moir, and Dean Schultz were in attendance. I don't remember who else was in attendance, but the meeting was short and to the point.

"Why, Mr. Wiltz?" asked Captain Moir.

"I have no respect whatsoever for some of the officer candidates you have recruited. Many are excellent, but there are those who couldn't lead a brownie scout field trip."

"Mr. Wiltz, I know exactly who you are referring to, but I can tell you this. They will never get beyond the rank of captain," responded Captain Moir.

"A captain is an officer in the United States Army!" I replied. It was quiet for a moment.

"Mr. Wiltz has made an excellent point!" stated Dean Schultz. From that moment on, Dean Frank Schultz was "The Man" at SDSC as far as I was concerned.

They asked me to leave the room. Ten minutes later I was asked to return. If given a chance, would I fulfill my ROTC requirement without further incident? I was humble, and I was grateful for the opportunity. I did some serious growing up. On the way out, Dean Schultz called me aside. He wanted me to start reading Aldous Huxley. I don't know what he had in mind, but I will say that *Brave New World* helped shape my future thinking. Frank Schultz and I became friends.

In looking back, I was perhaps too critical not just of ROTC, but much of what was taking place around me. My skepticism found its way to Maynard Fox's American Literature class where the final exam asked us to take a hard, in depth look at Henry David Thoreau. Though I admired his "Civil Disobedience," I saw Thoreau as a Walden Pond dreamer lacking in initiative, and I said as much. My attitude nearly caused me to fail the required course. At this same time I also played a key role in hanging the president in effigy from a tree in front of the library.

It was indeed a troubled time. I was becoming increasingly fond of Betsy, and it was obvious that her parents, her mother especially, would do everything possible to drive us apart. My being from Chicago was a part of it as Betsy's father had been mugged in Chicago while attending a 4-H function.

My being a Catholic was an even bigger problem. I do not doubt that catholic-protestant conflicts existed in 1962, and I do not doubt that both sides fueled the fire equally. However, in my twelve years of catholic school education, I never heard a negative word about my protestant brothers and sisters. We would go to the same heaven. We worshipped the same God. The parental animosity that Betsy tolerated was very wrong. Jesus Christ preached loving our neighbors. What Betsy endured was inexcusable.

The 1962 SDSC campus was somewhat of a melting pot as there were a number of foreign students from China, India, and the Arab nations. It prompted me to join the International Relations Club where I attended a number of supper meetings. One particular guest speaker left a lasting impression in my mind. He was extremely critical of the many foreign students who sought American citizenship. While it may have been their original intent to take their education home and help their own people, too many would abandon their noble plans in his opinion. He laid it on them.

The third floor of East Mens Hall came under the influence of my little friend from Beirut, Lebanon, Farouk Dejani. Farouk was comical but demanding. He often approached me or someone who owned a car.

"You will take me downtown!" He demanded.

"Bull shit!" We shouted back. I suspect that Farouk was accustomed to servants.

Cultures have their differences. An Arab dorm room smelled like lightening had struck the dairy building, and it seemed that every Arab room had a dishpan full of sour milk on top of the radiator. Was it some sort of cheese? I often saw sandal tracks on the toilet seat, and I presumed that my Arab friends squatted on the seat with their sandals on. Who's to say which way was best? At the time I wondered about Arab women and the toilet seats in the women's dorm rooms. In looking back now, there were no Arab women in school.

During that 1962-1963 school year in Brookings, my life was twice threatened on the telephone. My own thoughtlessness fostered the first encounter.

For the sake of identification, I had stupidly drawn a swastika on the cover of my German notebook. I was called and asked if I was a Nazi. Though I emphatically denied it, I was asked to prove it, and told that I might be killed if I was indeed a Nazi. The caller identified himself as a John Birch Society member. I immediately destroyed my notebook cover. A year later I heard that Brookings John Birchers cheered the assassination of President Kennedy.

I saw the second incident as somewhat humorous. SDSC's largest lecture room with theatre seats might have been in the west end of Ag Hall. During an Econ class lecture, a girl on the opposite side of class asked a question. In asking, she said she was from Chicago. After class I waited for her by the door as I was curious about where she was from. We walked together for a block or two before parting ways.

A phone call interrupted my afternoon nap.

"Hallo. Is dis Roger Walz?" It was obviously some foreign student as he pronounced Roger with a soft "G."

"Yes!" I answered in an amused tone of voice.

"You will leave my wife alone or I will keel you!" he shouted.

"Hey guy! You must be crazy! I've never messed with anyone's wife!" I shouted back. And then I hung up. I wondered for days what the wife thing was all about. A week later, while in the same Ag Hall Econ class, a folded note worked its way to me. It read,

"I'm so sorry. Please excuse my husband and the ways of his country. He is possessive to the point it causes problems for me."

I looked around the room and spotted the Chicago girl I had talked to. When she signaled me with a very modest wave, I finally understood. Neither John Birch nor the foreign student ever threatened me again.

At this same time my mother's health was deteriorating. Janet, my fourteen-year-old sister, along with my father, were caring for my bed-ridden mother as well as handling household chores. These included getting Mike, my six-year-old brother, off to school. While Dad's life was either work or the home front, he did have an hour or two after prepping Mom for bed….. a 24-7 task that included bathing and dressing bedsores. Through a co-worker, Dad had become interested in Model A Fords. He gave me an assignment: Find him a restorable Model A.

By scouring the countryside for pheasants and antique Fords at the same time, I covered a lot of ground. My first Model A was a 1929 two-door sedan I spotted in a pasture southeast of Bruce, SD. While the farmer who owned it had no emotional attachment to the car, he said he used it to round up his cattle. I offered to trade him the 1948 Plymouth I was driving, and we made a deal. I immediately replaced my Plymouth with a 1950 Dodge I bought from a local dealer for fifty dollars. Brother John and I towed the Ford to Chicago behind the Dodge.

As Dad worked on a ground up restoration of the chassis in the garage, he asked me to keep an eye out for a more popular body style. My next Model A was a 1930 Town Sedan I drove to Chicago. I paid $125 for that car. In the end, Dad fully restored a 1929 rumble sear Sport Coupe that came from the Willow Lake, SD area. The $200 I paid was a good chunk of money at the time.

By the middle of my third year at SDSC, I began to realize there was a light at the end of the tunnel. I had a major that satisfied me, and I was beginning to see myself as a South Dakotan. It was during spring football that I became increasingly aware of the fact that no matter how hard I worked and how much I liked football, I would probably never make second team let alone first. I was and always will be proud of the fact that I was on a very good championship football team. I thought about resetting some priorities.

<u>Senior Year</u> 1963-1964

When J.B. and I headed to Brookings in the fall of '63, we had no place to stay. While Student Housing gave us an "approved list" of off-campus possibilities, a newspaper ad brought us to 611 6th Street, the very modest home of Harry and Nettie Dingman.

"Spartan" might be a good way to describe the small upstairs rooms, but the price was right. Ten dollars a month to share a room, and twelve dollars for a private suite. My private room looked out over 6th Street. JB would share a room in the back. The "Throne Room" was the size of a broom closet, and when seated on the throne, one's knees held the door open. We would share the downstairs bathtub with the Dingman's. J.B. and I would soon be joined at Dingman's by South Dakotans Roger Ensenbach of Sioux Falls, John Janes of Wessington Springs, and Dave Robbins of White.

Harry and Nettie were precious. They were married in a country church at the stroke of midnight 1900. How cool was that! In a short time we were calling Nettie "Granny." We called Harry "Gramps" to his face, but among ourselves he was "Old Rivers." I could write a book about the Dingman's, and there's a story about them in my book, *A Dakota Rod and Nimrod*.

Classes were going well, and along with a smattering of most every subject offered, I took a few education courses although being a teacher was far from my mind. I did fall under the influence of Les Forman and Marvin Scholten – great educators. I had also taken some coaching classes that included baseball, basketball, football, track & field, and wrestling. Jim Iverson, Jim Marking, Stan Marshall, and Warren Williamson were great coaches and role-models.

As you will soon learn, my future profession included evaluating high school teachers and attempting to improve their classroom effectiveness.

Did university department heads evaluate the classroom performance of their instructors, associate professors, and professors? Is tenure protecting "dead wood"? I have pondered this question for many years.

During the 1963-1964 school year, I took Shakespeare, a required course for my English major. Joseph Giddings was my instructor. While Giddings knew his subject matter well enough, my only concern was that our final grade was based on one exam – the semester final. I received a "B" on the exam and a "B" for the course. Fair enough. It was the grade I deserved.

There were perhaps a dozen girls in the class. I was the only guy. While checking my grade on the bulletin board outside the department office, a few of the girls asked me about my grade. I had the only "B." The girls received "A's." The girls congratulated me on my honest effort. The Giddings Shakespeare final was on file in the girls' dorm, and it hadn't changed in many years. I didn't know. I do know that Giddings was far from being over-worked.

As mentioned, I've pondered questions about college education for much of my life. Beginning in 1960, summer jobs more than paid for my college education. Since then, the cost of a college education has risen exponentially, and today's grads are often left in substantial debt. What happened?

During the summer of 1964, while I was working in the steel mill, Betsy called me one night. She was sobbing, and she said that she couldn't take it anymore. Her parents were relentless with regard to me. Betsy was worth fighting for!

I took off the following morning in my1950 Dodge at 4:00 A.M. and headed for Huron, SD.....Betsy's home. I walked into the kitchen at supper time and asked, "What's your problem with my God?" When the smoke cleared, Betsy's father, Merlin, was in my corner. Our romantic crisis was now ever so gradually becoming more tolerable.

Fall 1964

I had been accepted to the SDSC graduate school on probation, no doubt because of my GPA, and in looking back, I was fortunate to have been accepted at all. I knew that Betsy and I would probably marry in the not too distant future, and I knew Chicago was not a part of her future plans. What would I do as a South Dakotan?

I was considering a McDonald's franchise for Brookings, and a Brookings bank was willing to finance the endeavor. I was also thinking about teaching-coaching although not too seriously. I enrolled in the "Ed-Block" that included student teaching, and I was placed in Arlington, SD where I taught high school English. It went well enough. Arlington superintendent Amos Tschetter offered me a full-time position. During this time Betsy entered her junior year as an English major.

John Janes, a fellow resident at the Dingman home the previous year, and I rented a room from Felix Shaw, an Econ professor. Felix, aka Harrison Hsia, also rented a room in his Faculty Drive home to some Chinese students. I'll always remember the Friday night before the pheasant opener when John and I got out our shotguns to clean them in the living room. The Chinese, who usually controlled the TV set, disappeared for the rest of the evening. What had they experienced in their past?

At this same time, the ROTC Department at the college sponsored a youth boy's basketball league. ROTC supplied the team shirts, and games were played at the downtown armory. I volunteered to coach, and John, my roommate, volunteered to co-coach with me. It was a good experience, and it proved that my one-time strained relationship with ROTC was healed. Those 5th-6th grade boys were a challenge.

Willow Lake, SD

During this time period I received a call from the English Department. It would prove to be a life-defining event. The Willow Lake High School had an English teacher resign for health reasons, and the school needed a teacher for the second semester. Would SDSC help find a replacement? I told the department that I would look into it.

I made the sixty mile drive to the northwest and met with Supt. Jack Titus. He was likeable, and I had come to like small towns. The state would grant an "authority to act" for the coursework I lacked, and I signed a contract for half of the $4500 base salary. I could make that much in ten weeks at the steel mill, but my decision wasn't about money. Might teaching be a good career choice? I now had the opportunity to take a close look.

Upon my return to Willow Lake on the Sunday prior to the beginning of the 2nd semester, I rented a room in the home of John and Mae Meester for $15 a month. The Meesters were an elderly retired couple, and Mae went out of her way to make me understand that meals weren't included......with the exception of supper that night and breakfasts on most mornings – a temporary arrangement you understand. When I got home in the late afternoon, there were usually some fresh-baked goods waiting for me.

When I went out to my car the following morning in minus twenty degree temperatures, all four of my tires were flat! Welcome to Willow Lake Mr. Wiltz!

I walked up to the school and told Mr. Titus to rip up my contract. I didn't need this, I had offended no one, and I would take some grad courses second semester in Brookings and be near Betsy.

"Will you give it a day?" asked Mr. Titus.

"No way!" I replied.

"Will you give us an hour?" begged Mr. Titus.

"What will we do in an hour?" I asked.

"We will have an assembly with the high school students. I'll introduce you, and you can tell them why you're leaving," Offered Mr. Titus.

"I can do that," I answered. I was upset, and I could certainly give them the "what for."

The old gym was in the basement, and we stood on a stage on the south end. One could have heard a pin drop after I spoke. In the back I could see four guys getting to their feet. They came forward.

"We did it, Mr. Wiltz, and we're sorry. Please give us a chance. If any of your tires are ruined, we'll get you new ones."

They were sincere. I couldn't turn my back on them, and by noon that day I knew what I wanted to do.....probably for the rest of my life.

During that 2nd semester at Willow Lake, I coached a one-act play and we won a contest. I had never been in a play in my life. I also introduced some of the guys to wrestling, and I helped some of the shot-putters on the powerful Willow Lake track team. I signed a contract for the 1965-1966 school year, and my duties would include high school English, German, head-wrestling, and assistant football as well as junior class adviser. I also rented a farm home a mile south of town that would serve as Roger and Betsy's first home.

During our first summer of married life, I coached American Legion Baseball, VFW Teener baseball, the midgets, and the pee-wees. I "lived" at the ball park as I mowed the entire field with our hand push mower and coached all day. On the Monday morning after our Saturday wedding and Sunday Sioux Falls honeymoon, the midgets and pee-wees were knocking at our back door by 8:00 A.M. wanting me for baseball. The Legion team was a force with the likes of Jim Thoreson and the late Ron Johnson.

Betsy and I were married in Brookings at the St. Thomas Moore Church on June 12, 1965 by father Richard Mahowald, the priest at the campus Newman Center. Father Mahowald, a great man, brought everyone together in harmony on our special day as Willow Lake students cheered from the balcony.

**Wedding picture with Betsy's parents Merlin & Evelyn
Hodgson, Betsy, Roger, and my father, John.**

As we settled into our first year of married life at Willow Lake, Betsy began her senior year on the SDSC campus by taking the education block. She would student teach at nearby Lake Norden and drive to our

Willow Lake home at the end of her school day. She was also pregnant with our first child. We had promised her parents that our marriage would not disrupt her education plans, and she was determined to keep that promise.

My teaching career began smoothly enough. I loved the classroom. Other than my recent student teaching experience, I didn't have much to go on for teaching ideas other than weekly writing assignments, striving for improvement, and reading quality literature.

In the *Forward* to this book, I alluded to my career as an educator spanning a time of transition. This was certainly evident at Willow Lake where the superintendent told us goose hunters that if we got into a flock of geese before school in the morning, we could stay with them as he would supervise our students in study hall until we returned. We could simply put our shotguns in the school shop. Those days are gone forever.

Willow Lake was blessed with a good number of exceptional athletes, and football went very well under head coach Larry Donovan. Larry let me handle the defense, and I was comfortable with that to the point I invited SDSU head coach Ralph Ginn and his staff to Willow Lake to watch the Pirates end Howard's 28 game winning streak. Willow Lake won 12-0.

I made my football coaching debut the night we played Lake Preston at Lake Preston. Coach Larry was sick, and I was a nervous wreck. As the team and I waited on the bus for the driver, the team informed me that I was the driver. That was my first bus driving experience. We won 34-0. More important, we got home safely.

Willow Lake's 1st year wrestling team did well as we knocked off arch-rival Clark and took down Doland twice in a bitter rivalry that the school boards mutually ended. I had much to learn, and I was already regretting my quitting SDSC's fine wrestling program. Darwin Grimm was my ticket to my first state wrestling tournament.

The Accident

On Sunday morning, January 23rd, 1966, we were coming home from Church at Bryant when I stopped our new Dodge pickup at the junction of Highways 25 and 28. I rolled down my window and looked south down Hwy 25, but I didn't see the silver-colored Buick in the blowing snow. When I pulled on to the highway we were broadsided by the Buick going 70 mph.

The car struck the left side of my driver's side door and pushed the door into the cab. Through the opening I sailed over the intersection, over the fence, and landed unconscious in a cattail slough. The first people on the scene placed a blanket over my body. My body was unscathed. Betsy was less fortunate. The blow drove her left temple onto the steering wheel, a blow that would permanently cause loss of her left eye.

I vividly remember sitting up in a slough and pulling a blanket off of my body. I couldn't imagine what was going on until I saw our pickup thirty yards away in the same slough.

Miraculously, the Steen family in the Buick only suffered cuts and bruises. Betsy and I were taken to the Sioux Falls McKennan Hospital by ambulance. Betsy, unconscious, was placed in ICU. They kept me a few days for observation purposes.

When I was dismissed, they encouraged me to return to my teaching job at Willow Lake. On the morning of my first day back, the hospital called the school. Betsy's vital signs were plummeting, and I had to get to the hospital to sign papers for surgery. I received a 110 mph police car ride back to Sioux Falls.

There was fluid on Betsy's brain, and they had to go after the clot by cutting holes in her head. It was educated guesses and trial and error, but the second hole was right on though she remained unconscious.

Within the week, Betsy, who was approximately seven months pregnant, went into labor. I was told that Betsy, in her weakened condition, would not survive the rigors of labor. They also told me the baby had a 50/50 chance. Betsy was in labor for only 15 minutes.

As labor was much shorter than anticipated, Betsy came through. With the baby off of her system, Betsy slowly regained consciousness. They pressed me to name the baby, and I chose Laurie Dawn.

Because Laurie Dawn at 4 lbs. 10 oz began losing weight, they placed her on a soy bean formula under the supervision of Sister Basil, a McKennan institution.

I brought baby Laurie home before Betsy was dismissed, and my nightly duties other than grading papers included bottling formula and washing diapers. When Laurie cried at night, I rocked her cradle with my left foot as I lay in bed and talked to her.

To say the Willow Lake community truly rose to the occasion is an understatement. Most everyone wanted to give me a car. I left off a bundled baby Laurie before school, along with formula and diapers, with an assortment of families. The "volunteer" list was long. In the meantime, I was off to Sioux Falls in borrowed vehicles whenever time permitted.

When Betsy eventually came home, life returned to a normal pace. Her final semester of school would go on hold until the summer of 1970 when I received a Masters Degree and Betsy her Bachelors after we spent a summer session on campus.

As much as we loved Willow Lake and its people, we began to think about living in a community that had doctors. DeSmet and the great Doctor Bell were 35 miles away. The Parkston, SD school was looking for an English teacher and someone to start a wrestling program, and I applied for the position and was offered the job.

Leaving Willow Lake was an emotional experience. Upon our return to town after an American Legion baseball game in Estelline, SD, the entire Willow Lake community met us at the Four Mile Corner east of town where we joined the parade that headed for the city park and a community picnic – good luck celebration where we were presented with gifts. There were tears in my eyes when we pulled out of our driveway for the last time.

During this past year Betsy and I attended the Willow Lake Class of 1967's 50th reunion where we had a great time.

The Parkston, SD Years - 1966-1971

At the time of our Willow Lake – Parkston transition, Betsy's father, Merlin Hodgson, was terminally ill with cancer in his sinuses. The probable cause was his working with herbicides and pesticides in his county agent position. Merlin was a participant in the WWII Normandy Invasion, but modest as he was, he never talked about it.

My mother, Lucille, was also bed-ridden and frail with multiple sclerosis. Neither parent would survive our first year at Parkston.

Our move brought us from Willow Lake's brutally northern clime to what seemed like a "banana belt." We rented the Vernon Tiede farm house four miles east of Parkston – a wonderful place for our girls to spend their earliest years.

That peaceful farm setting once caused some anxious moments. We discovered one summer morning that baby Lisa was missing. After a quick once-through of the house, we summoned the Tiedes for help.

The southwest corner of the yard was a feedlot full of black white-faced cattle. I can still picture Lisa's tiny legs in the midst of the herd. I dashed into the lot and scooped her up. When I asked her what she was doing, she replied, "Talking to the cows."

Parkston had a prosperous business climate along with three fine family doctors – Doctors McCann, Monson, and Porter. I would also soon recognize that I had become part of an excellent school system as I was surrounded by some great teachers.

My teaching position, funded by federal Title I funds, was both unique and challenging. The students in my freshmen, sophomore, junior, and senior English classes were the 20% with the lowest language arts scores on standardized tests. I feared that the students in the regular English classes might view my students as "Special Ed" students, and I was determined to make my students feel good about their placement. The title of my position, Remedial English, didn't help the situation. There was also an early incident that didn't help my cause.

Mrs. Ella Wittmeier taught English I. I don't know exactly what she said, but it came out that I was a good pick for Remedial English as I struggled with the subject matter myself. When I learned of this allusion from my students, I stormed into Mr. Wurtz's office, the principal, and asked him to send for Mrs. Wittmeier. When she came in, I slammed a twenty-dollar bill on the counter and told her to anti-up. We were going to take an English test, and Mr. Wurtz would officiate. I was angry, and the poor lady was terrified. She became an ally from that point on.

Other than state mandated curriculum, my students wrote essays on weekly assigned topics. Compositions were turned-in on Friday, new topics were assigned on Monday, and graded compositions were returned on Monday. Monday's syllabus always included the essay topic along with twenty vocabulary words taken from *Collegiate Word Power* published by Markhart. They were tested on these every Friday morning. If nothing else, I was organized.

My primary grammar emphasis came with their weekly writing assignments. When I graded their papers, I underlined in red their problem areas. It was their responsibility to correct their own errors with a hint or assistance from me. Title I required that I pre-test and post-test my students. They made significant measurable progress, and I was shocked to learn just how effective my method of instruction was.

Title I afforded me a comfortable operating budget. I used much of it to buy paperback novels as well as financing field trips. For example,

I required my juniors to read Upton Sinclair's *The Jungle*. For a field trip, we visited the John Morrell packing plant in Sioux Falls. The sophomores read Rolvaag's *Giants in the Earth*. With this we did a James River float trip and examined a genuine sod hut. The freshmen read Orwell's *Animal Farm* and studied both satire and the Russian Revolution. My Title I students worked hard, and they profited from it.

Other than my coaching responsibilities, my psychology class elective gave me the opportunity to work with all Parkston students. I felt that my research project assignment was innovative, and my students certainly got into it. After studying measuring instruments including popular intelligence tests, I gave them a background in statistics including mean, median, mode, standard deviation, correlation and scales such as the Likert. They created their own measuring devices, and established experimental and control groups. One boy built an effective Skinner box. My biggest problem was holding them back. Some saw themselves as a Masters and Johnson! Our reading Huxley's *Brave New World* no doubt gave birth to this thinking.

After serving as assistant football coach during my first three years at Parkston, I was named head coach. I'm proud to say that we (assistant coaches Gene Garry and Gene Zulk) turned the program into a winner immediately.

The new wrestling program went well as we more or less dominated the conference after our first year. In 1971, we were runner-up in the state tournament. I would one day during the 1997-1998 school year be inducted into the South Dakota Wrestling Hall of Fame. Being recognized by my peers was a great honor of which I am very proud.

The late sixties were a troubled time of protest and civil disobedience. The Viet Nam War fostered a climate that filtered down to the best of our high school students. I remember our high school band marching out of the building to protest the music director Ron Hilgenberg was asking them to play. Someone had called in the media. Ron was a great teacher and a great man, and I really felt for Ron as the incident was a travesty. Ron retired at the end of the 68-69 school year to do volunteer work for his church. He was killed on the Interstate by a drive-by shooter. The Lord's ways are not for us to understand.

Parkston was a farm community, and support for the sometimes violent NFO, National Farmers Organization, was readily apparent in some of my students.

Midway through my Parkston tenure, one of those life-defining moments came along. I came home grumbling to Betsy about faculty meetings for the sake of meetings. Why not have a meeting when we need to talk about something? Betsy's response was monumental. "Maybe you should be the principal."

At this same time, State, now known as SDSU, was offering extension graduate courses in nearby Mitchell. I began work on a Masters Degree.

Our middle daughter, Lisa Marie, was born in Parkston on August 23rd, 1967. Betsy, by our choice, was a "stay at home mom." I find it interesting that on my $4900 salary, we were comfortable.

During the summer of 1969, I did a session on the SDSU campus to work on my Masters. During the summer of 1970, both Betsy and I did an SDSU summer session. Betsy completed her Bachelors Degree and I my Masters in School Administration. We hired Kathy Tiede, who lived across the road, to care for Laurie and Lisa. Kathy did a splendid job as the girls loved her.

With my Masters degree in hand, it was decision time – remain in the classroom or take an administrative position. We chose administration.

The Burke, SD Years — 1971-1976

Because of the hunting and fishing, I wanted to live in Gregory County. I had also become friends with Jerry Opbroek, the Burke wrestling coach and one of the most gifted teachers I've ever known. Gregory County met with Betsy's approval, and I applied for two positions in Gregory County — Superintendent at Fairfax and High School Principal/Guidance Counselor at Burke. I was offered both positions.

I was giving the Fairfax position serious consideration when it fell apart. I told the school board that we were four miles away from neighboring Bonesteel on a paved highway, and even though it might cost me my job, I would work to bring the two districts together. A chill came over the room. It was all over. Fairfax made the Burke decision for me.

We liked Burke from the start. It was a wonderful place to live. Laurie started kindergarten that first fall. We bought our first home with an FHA loan for $6000 in the spring of 1972, and under the guidance of Art Jones, the industrial arts teacher, we built a garage that same summer. LuAnn Michelle, our youngest daughter, was born on November 15, 1971, and Lisa entered kindergarten in the fall of '72. Betsy and I will be forever grateful for the outstanding staff of elementary teachers that gave our girls a solid educational foundation.

My administrative career got off to a rocky start. About the second week of school, Audrey Brevik, the elementary principal, came to me with a serious problem. 5th grade band members were missing math class in the morning because they had been placed in the high school band - no doubt to build numbers. I gave the importance of 5th grade math, with its introduction to fractions, about three seconds of thought and told Miss Brevik that the 5th graders would be in math the following morning.

I then went to see our band instructor. Surely she would have no problem with my decision. I couldn't have been more mistaken. She told me that when she got through with me, her daddy would see to it that the 5th graders would be back in band, and I wouldn't have a job. Well, the 5th graders went to math, and I was still the principal a week later. I hope she can laugh about it today.

A miserable failure still plagues me today. None of my college guidance & counseling classes prepared me for what was about to happen.

One of my high school students came into my office and pleaded for help. The student feared being alcoholic, and confided in me that it was difficult to carry on without a drink.

I was blown away to the point I couldn't react. I didn't know young people could be alcoholic, and I didn't know that Teen Alcoholics Anonymous existed. I completely failed that student. I was as green as a counselor could be. I only hope that today's school guidance counselors have a solid background in helping young people deal with addiction.

In looking back, my role as guidance counselor was not a total failure. I successfully encouraged a senior boy during my first year to apply for a four-year General Motors scholarship which he received. Two other young men were admitted to West Point and the Air Force Academy respectively. We also made progress at raising ACT scores.

My effectiveness as a Burke administrator was hampered by my accepting too many roles. Following Jerry Opbroek's move to Mitchell,

SD, I was named head wrestling coach beginning with the 1972-1973 school year. I coached junior high football, and I taught German and creative writing. Because of Superintendent John Frank's failing health, I was appointed acting superintendent. Overseeing the schools at Herrick and Lucas was also time consuming. The school board may have viewed me as an easy solution with the coaching positions, but I should have said "No" to these roles.

My flair for innovation became apparent in my German II class. In an SDSU Methods of Teaching class, Dr. Maynard Cochrane advocated Individualized Instruction through the use of what he called "Capsules" or "Uni-Packs." The packets I developed included pre and post-tests along with instruction. Students worked at their own rate. While I had a few students who excelled to a mid-German III level, most lagged behind. While my effort may have been commendable, it was an overall failure.

During the latter part of my Burke tenure, the school board made me spokesperson for a bond issue that included a new gymnasium and classroom complex in Burke, as well as closing the learning centers in Lucas and Herrick. While I was personally sold on the merits of the project, it only served to create enemies. The bond issue failed the first time around.

I learned a huge lesson. Point out the pros and cons of an issue, but let the decision to close a school come from the local people. Don't ram it down their throats!

There is a happy ending to this story. I feel that the greatest honor of my life was giving the 1977 graduation address in the new Burke gymnasium. A lot of good money has been thrown at bad relative to struggling school districts and building projects, but Burke's decision has proven to be right on. I mentioned Fairfax and Bonesteel at the beginning of this chapter. Today they are one.

During my Burke years, I became very involved in officiating wrestling. It involved collegiate matches at USD-Springfield for Mike Durfee as well as Yankton College at Yankton. I officiated in Nebraska from Boy's Town to Chadron. I enjoyed it, and it was a welcome supplement to our income.

While at Burke, I became aware of the presence of South Dakota's reservation system. Fishing trips to the Rosebud with Art Jones was a part of it, as was being a member of Governor Kneip's "Task Force for Peace." AIM (American Indian Movement) had stirred things up to the point that it was difficult not to be aware of the unrest.

I've mentioned Art Jones. Art was our Burke High School shop teacher. A popular shop class activity was building black powder rifles. Times have indeed changed.

One of my life's defining moments occurred one morning before school on a stockdam bank just east of Burke. I had caught a big bass, and Pries Fahrenbacker, publisher of *The Burke Gazette,* heard about it. He took a photo and asked me to write a short account of the event. That story generated a weekly column that I have written for the past 47 years. That column also gave birth to my first book, *A Dakota Rod and Nimrod.*

In the spring of 1976 I resigned my position at Burke. I applied for two positions – High School Principal at Wagner, SD and High School Principal at Sundance, Wyoming.

The Sundance or Crooks County school board narrowed their over one hundred applicants to twelve hour-long weekend interviews. Among the many questions they asked of me was, "Are extra-curricular activities a right or a privilege?" Good Question. I was offered the position, but there was no available housing in Sundance. The shortage related to mining activities. Betsy was also a bit cool about moving farther away from family, and we passed on the Sundance opportunity.

I was offered the Wagner position, and we were familiar with Wagner as it was an SESD conference school as were both Parkston and Burke. I knew Supt. Dale Hall as we attended SDSU summer sessions together, and I knew many of the Wagner coaches including Tom Studelska.

Wagner was closer to Betsy's family in Sioux Falls, and I'll admit that Wagner's new school building was attractive. At the time I had it in my mind that "bigger was better," (not true at all), and I believed that success at Wagner could land me most any position I wanted. I took the Wagner position.

Book III – The Wagner Years 1976 – Present

A Brief Job Description and My First Year

We moved into a house we rented from the Wagner school on July 4th, 1976. By mid-week I was in my office working on schedules.

The job title, High School Principal, was misleading. Grades 7-12, along with classrooms, staff, and bell schedule, were combined. I never thought about the enormity of the job at the time, but scheduling and supervising 300 high school students, 150 junior high students, evaluating 28 staff members, and attending all events including athletics and music generally called for a twelve hour day. Sunday afternoons in the office were almost mandatory.

Attendance, especially with junior high Native American students, was the greatest challenge by far. Determining exactly who legal guardians were compounded the problem. When all efforts failed, signing a "failure to send child to school" complaint led to an appearance before Judge Paul Kern in the county court house. I didn't have time to spend afternoons in court, and establishing priorities was paramount. Attendance was paramount as absence spelled failure.

Fortunately, Wednesday nights, "Church Night," were sacred. Teaching religion classes was something I had done since the Willow Lake days when all the Catholic students met in our living room on Wednesday nights. At Parkston we met in the old parish elementary school, and in Burke we met in the church which was across the street from our home. I had 33 consecutive years of Wednesday nights before I gave that up – largely due to my hearing problem.

My early Wagner school years were graced with artists and professionals funded by The National Endowments for the Arts. I'll never forget the time Supt. Dale Hall, Elementary Principal Evelyn Rueb, and I were sent to a modern dance festival at Cape Cod Community College to learn about modern dance and how to incorporate a modern dance company into our curriculum. We were cautioned that some of our home communities might not accept nude dance presentations very well. Amen!

One dance session stands out in my mind. Entwined with a partner, we were to imagine ourselves as a melting chunk of ice. I took a chair immediately. Unfortunately for her, some girl half my size approached and asked me to be her partner. I ultimately collapsed on her and nearly crushed her.

Artists I recall include the great Mark Howard, a Broadway music producer (I still marvel at what he accomplished and got out of our kids), and writers Freya Manfred and Linda Hasselstrom.

Beginning in the spring of 1977 there was a brutal period of "burning the candle at both ends." We bought an acreage two miles north of town and embarked on a housing project. After Francis Doom's Wagner Building Supply poured a basement and framed up a house, we took over.

My father did all the plumbing and wiring while I did insulation, dry wall, woodwork, carpeting, painting, and building a laundry room, bathroom, two bedrooms, and a rec room in the basement. We moved into the house to save rent money while our construction projects were in progress!

I also built a cinder block chimney and cut a chimney hole through the foundation wall for the Fisher wood-burning stove that would heat the house. Cutting firewood on Sunday afternoons while the girls and Betsy loaded the pickup became a family activity.

Parents and Discipline

Wagner High School was a great school, and all great schools have good discipline. It must be consistent and "color" free. Students knew the consequences of their actions, and I don't recall a student ever feeling that he/she had been treated unfairly. Parents were a different matter – a situation that became progressively worse. Many of today's parents try to shield their children from consequences and accountability. These ingredients must be a part of growing into responsible adulthood. The one area where parents had the biggest problem dealing with school discipline was alcohol.

Incidents involving alcohol were not frequent over my 21 years as principal, but they rose from time to time. I was a bit naïve "alcohol wise" when I began at Wagner, but I learned quickly.

As previously mentioned, I was a Wednesday night religious instruction teacher at Wagner's St. John the Baptist Catholic Church. A program featuring Teen AA or Alcoholics Anonymous was brought in from Yankton, and one of the presenters told me that I was a fool if I didn't realize that alcohol was being consumed in our school on a daily basis. Though I took offense to the remark, I soon learned the Teen AA'ers knew what they were talking about.

Concerning alcohol in school, school policy included calling in parents/guardians. The first offense included suspension time and loss of some privileges. The consequences of a second offense could involve expulsion, but I don't recall any second time offenders. School policy apparently worked.

One particularly ugly situation came about when I chanced upon a girl in the school parking lot who was drinking orange vodka straight from the bottle. In my office her parents were screaming at me that their daughter didn't drink while at the same time the girl was screaming at her parents that she had a drinking problem.

In my 21 years as principal, the school board backed my handling of discipline on every occasion with the exception of the time they took one of my most effective "weapons" away after a very trying ordeal.

The study hall supervisor reported that four boys who had signed out for the library weren't in the library. I found them in the parking lot standing around a pickup truck. A cooler full of beer was in the truck's box.....a cause for suspicion. When a slight breeze came up, a beer can rolled out from under the truck. I escorted the boys to my office.

The smell of alcohol was easy to detect in my confined office. When the boys denied drinking, I took my breathilizer out of my desk drawer. All four boys tested positive. I called the parents.

While some of the parents were more upset with their sons than me, some were absolutely livid over my having the breathilizer. Those same parents must have tormented the school board to the point where the board instructed me to get the breathilizer out of the school.

That breathilizer had been extremely effective. The kids knew I had it, and it definitely made prom supervision an easier task. On more than one occasion during evening activities, I saw kids turn around on the sidewalk when they saw me by the door.

Up to a point, many parents condoned alcohol. As they often said, "At least it isn't drugs." Some parents actually hosted pre-prom alcohol consumption parties. Some of the parents who chaperoned a school band excursion became almost hostile when I banned their drinking and beer coolers on the bus.

To this day I wonder whether or not parents want an alcohol-free school. Apparently they didn't when I was the principal.

The Fire

I'm guessing that it was January 1979. Betsy and I were awakened about 3:00 a.m. by Brown, our Chesapeake Bay Retriever, who was barking beneath our bedroom window. She might have saved our lives. An orange glow came from our north window, and when I looked out, I could see that our pole barn was engulfed in flames.

We roused the girls and called the fire department. The Wagner Volunteer Fire Department arrived within minutes and in my estimation, saved our home that was dangerously close to the burning barn. Brown lost her puppies, and we lost Morris the cat. We also lost my fully restored 1929 Model A Ford Sport Coupe, our fully restored Model A John Deere tractor, and our Pipestone fishing boat.

The following morning, the state fire marshal stopped by my office. He informed me that I hadn't started the fire as I would have first removed the Model A Ford. I didn't appreciate his thinking. The Ford had been a gift from my father – priceless! The Ford was uninsured. The fire marshal hadn't yet determined the cause. That night Laurie and Lisa told me about the "nest" they had built for Brown that included bales, a heat lamp, and a blanket draped over it.

B & R Enterprises

During the summer of 1982, Bob and Carla Osterday came to Wagner in search of housing. Bob had signed on to teach American History and Jr. High social studies as well as serving as the head high school football coach. I had offered to help them find a place to live.

Rayburn Rueb, a local attorney, was showing us a house near the north end of Main Street. Though a rental price had been agreed upon, Rueb persisted in an effort to sell the house. For conversation's sake, I asked, "How much?" Rueb replied, "Make an offer." With the monthly rent figure in mind, I kicked some numbers around in my head.

"I'll give six-thousand if the owner will finance me at 6% for five years," I offered.

"You just bought a house!" replied Rayburn. My stomach knotted up. I had no intension of buying a house. After parting with the Osterdays, I headed up to the bank to consult with George Smith. To quote George,

"Wiltz, you done good. You'll pay for the house and put a few bucks in your pocket every month." That's how I figured it, but I needed reassurance.

Betsy and I opened a new account, B&R Enterprises (Betsy & Roger), and we never touched our regular checking account for anything rental related. Before long, we had rental properties all over town as well as a head start on rentals with incoming teachers. B&R funds eventually funded the kids' educations. The income was nice, but every penny was hard-earned – especially in the later years. We eventually helped some people get started with home ownership through "contract for deed" arrangements.

Wagner High School's Finest Hour

Today I often marvel at the level of patriotism displayed by Americans during World War II. The premier athletes of the day put their careers on hold to serve in the military. Ted Williams comes to mind. It seemed to me that this love of country was sorely missing in today's society.

Five Wagner High School senior boys made me realize that the sense of allegiance I longed to see in today's youth could be aroused by an act of aggression not unlike the bombing of Pearl Harbor.

On October 23, 1983, two suicide truck bombs crashed into a Beirut, Lebanon U.S. Marine barracks and killed 241 people including 220 Marines and 18 sailors. In the high school commons area that morning, fearful students confronted me and asked if they might be drafted into service. Five senior boys came up to me and said that we had to meet in my office right now! It was urgent.

The five boys – Tom Moysis, Robert Peters, Brad Novak, Terry Novak, and Steve Woods, told me, "No one does this to Americans and gets by with it." They informed me that they were quitting school immediately and joining the Marines. They wanted my support and approval.

We talked. I told them that I had never been prouder of any students – past and present. I tried to persuade them to wait until after graduation. Going right now would serve no practical purpose. They eventually agreed.

I'm very proud to report that all five boys did enlist in the Marine

Corps. I'm also proud to add that during my tenure at Wagner High, the student attitude toward the military was high. I give credit for that to Dana Sanderson, one of our counselors, as well as the professional ethics of the local recruiters. The presence of the local National Guard unit was also a factor as well as strong local VFW and American Legion chapters.

1992 picture of Laurie, LuAnn, and Lisa

The Wiltz Girls

It was a Saturday morning in early May of 1984. Rain had postponed the Avon track meet, and I saw it as a chance to help Laurie work on the discus. I had painted both discus and shotput circles on our driveway's concrete slab, and we had a place to practice. A light rain was falling, but it wasn't enough to curtail my plans.

As a junior, Laurie had placed in discus at the state meet, and I had visions of her winning state, and perhaps breaking the state record during her senior year.

During our workout, Laurie looked me in the eye as she started to speak. Were there tears in her eyes? No, it was probably the rain.

"Dad, when are you going to realize that this means a hell of a lot more to you than it means to me?"

We abruptly ended the practice session. As I related the incident to Betsy, I expected sympathy and consolation. A reprimand was all I received. It was time for some soul-searching.

Some years later I was the guest speaker at the Parkston High School athletic banquet where I related the above story. Following my presentation, a girl came up to me and thanked me. She, too, had tears in her eyes as she spoke.

"You'll never know how much my parents needed to hear what you said tonight."

I suspect that well-meaning parents like me too often try to relive their past through their children.

I see the following incident as perhaps one of the most significant messages in this book. I was and am so proud of our daughter, Lisa.

The office phone rang around nine o'clock. The call was for me, and it was the county sheriff. He wanted to know if Joanie Johnson was in school, and if she was, he would be by in half an hour to take her to juvenile detention in Sioux Falls. I checked the morning roll. Joanie was in school. I told the sheriff that he would have to have the necessary paper work before I would hand over any student. I also told him that he would not parade Joanie in front of the student body between bells. He should come to the office.

I went down to 8th grade Social Studies and asked Joanie to come with me. She came willingly and I was grateful as her behavior had been aggressive of late. We went into my office and I closed the door.

I told Joanie what was going to happen, and she accepted it without resistance. We had some time, and it looked like a good opportunity to talk. Joanie had been through some incredibly hard times, but if I reveal them, I'll reveal her identity.

"Joanie, do you have any friends in school?" I asked.

"One," she responded

"And who is that?" I questioned.

"Lisa Wiltz," she replied. "Do you know Lisa Wiltz?" What a silly question I thought to myself before it occurred to me that many of our kids don't know their fathers. Last names are meaningless.

"Yes, I know Lisa Wiltz," I answered. "Why is Lisa Wiltz your friend?" I asked.

"Because she smiles and says 'hello' to me in the hall," offered Joanie.

Her answer left me speechless. How could such an insignificant gesture make such a difference?

It was spring 1990. Our daughter, LuAnn, was a senior. She also happened to be president of the school's National Honor Society.

The honor society students wanted to wear sashes, or at least something, that would identify them as National Honor Society students at graduation. It was a fairly common practice in neighboring schools.

LuAnn presented her case to the school board, but the board wanted all graduates to appear as equals at graduation. Her request wasn't granted. As high school principal, it was my job to carry out school board policy.

Somehow a Sioux Falls television station got wind of the honor society issue, and they envisioned sitting down with honor society president LuAnn Wiltz and high school principal Roger Wiltz and taping a heated debate.

It never happened. LuAnn met the camera crew at the school's main entrance and told them to hit the road. Needless to say, I was very proud of LuAnn that day.

My Brother's Suicide

I feel that I made some mistakes with regard to my brother's suicide, and it is my hope that my failing can help a reader down the line. On the positive side, I can say that my suicide awareness increased dramatically, and that it served me as a school guidance counselor during my later days in education.

On February 18, 1997, my brother, John Byron, took his own life in Wauwatosa, WI, a Milwaukee suburb. We were close, and we often hunted or fished together. We often talked of the places we would go when retired. During our last hunt together in November 1996, I could see that he was troubled and we actually sat on a river bottom deadfall and talked about it with deer rifles in hand.

<u>Problem 1</u>: His employer, Wausau Insurance, was in the process of giving early retirement to some of its employees. A lucrative retirement package would be part of the deal. JB feared that he might be an early retiree. I responded that it was a dream come true as he could take the package and go with another company if he so desired.

<u>Problem 2</u>: JB owned a number of inner city rentals, many of them two and three flats. Some had turned into "crack" dens, and he feared that he might not be able to sell them when that day came. I asked him if his units had already paid for themselves, and he answered, "Many times over." I told him that if he had to let them go for taxes he was money ahead.

I made a serious mistake in down-playing his problems. His

problems may not have been problems in my eyes, but they were in his, and that's what mattered.

I also feel that there was a "red flag" in his final message to me that I completely missed. At the time he was recovering from eye surgery and was required to sit completely motionless for long periods of time. This, no doubt, contributed to his mental state. His home was also buried in the aftermath of a blizzard – a contributing situation. Judge his final message for yourself.

"12-21-96

Roger,

Surgery went o.k. and am home now and doing the best I can. It's a real challenge and the days so slow, bedtime is my favorite time of the day! Hope you received and am enjoying the gifts I sent. Merry Christmas!

J.B."

Jury Duty

Two or three times during my tenure as Wagner High School Principal I had been called to jury duty on the county level. Supt. Dale Hall felt that the school couldn't function without me, and he had apparently convinced the court of his feelings as I never received further notification.

At some later date I had read somewhere or heard it on television that securing good jurors was a major problem for our court system. The message struck home, and at that point I decided that I would cooperate, in spite of Supt. Hall's feelings, the next time called.

That "next time" was a notice to appear in the Sioux Falls federal courthouse. It would be one of the singular and most memorable events of my life.

As I recall, about sixty potential jurors had been called. The first day passed without my being questioned. During the afternoon session of the second day, I was half asleep when the prosecution called out loudly, "Roger Wiltz!" I hastily attempted to pull my thoughts together. I answered, "Here!"

"Mr. Wiltz, what if I were to tell you that the defendant might not take the stand during this trial?" asked the prosecution.

"I need a little time to think that over," I responded.

"Take all the time you need," said the prosecuting attorney.

After a lengthly pause I answered, "If one is presumed innocent until proven guilty, I guess it doesn't really matter."

"Very good Mr. Wiltz," replied the prosecution. I was never again addressed by the defense or the prosecution.

Following a series of peremptory challenges by both the prosecution and the defense, the jury was chosen by the end of the second day and I was to be a juror.

We jurors were sternly advised by the judge not to discuss any aspects of the trial with anyone – fellow jurors included. We readily complied. During the trial, crossing the street to Minerva's and back for lunch, and throughout the evening, we were guarded by armed U.S. marshals. In a brief conversation with one of them as we crossed Phillips Ave. for lunch, I asked if they were armed. After a reply in the affirmative, I asked with what. "A Glock" he replied.

The primary charge was the selling and distribution of illicit drugs. We listened to the testimony of perhaps 25 witnesses. Many of them were abusers trading testimony for jail time. I learned that I-90 was a major trafficking route, and that a truck stop in Rapid City was a popular exchange scene.

Some of the testimony included witnesses wearing "wires." Some of the exchanges occurred in ice-fishing shacks on Oahe, and the drugs had code names like "chartreuse spinners." Always there were times and dates.

I was elected jury foreman. In jury deliberation, we had to decide "guilty" or "not guilty" to the primary charge of selling and distributing, and then a dozen or so individual counts based on what, when, and where. When I first read the counts, I felt that we would never be able to remember dates and places. As it turned out, individual jurors were able to remember dates as they were significant dates in their own lives. We eventually charged "guilty" on all counts.

During the proceedings, I had wondered what the defense and prosecution attorneys knew about us as individual jurors. My question was answered when during the prosecutor's summation, he looked directly at me and said, "Whether you are a high school principal who belongs to Rotary….." They knew all about us.

After it was over, I left with the feeling that the man we convicted would probably be offered some kind of deal that might lead to the conviction of drug trafficking's "bigger fish." Jury duty is indeed an important part of American citizenship, and I am grateful for the opportunity that was given to me. When your name comes up, step up to the plate.

The School Bus Incident

To date, no incident in my life, other than the days that followed our January 1966 auto crash, has been as stressful and agonizing as the following that relates to my being the 7-12 principal at Wagner.

It was fall 1995, and the Wagner Red Raiders were playing a Friday night football game at Parkston, a distance of 40 miles from Wagner. As was typical, a student fan bus made the out-of-town trip.

I generally made all of the games, home and away, but I wasn't feeling well that evening, and I stayed home and went to bed early. The phone rang around 10:00 p.m. It was a fan bus student who had been left off the bus at her farm's driveway by Ray, the bus driver. She had been instructed to call me and ask me to meet the bus in the school parking lot.

I met the bus and climbed aboard. I was told by the bus chaperone that a number of students had left the game and gone into town where they had been caught stealing bicycles by the local police. I asked Lisa, the chaperone, if she knew who the students were who left the game. She knew, and she had made a list. We then dismissed the innocent students one by one. All of the remaining students happened to be Native American, but I don't know that that had entered my mind.

I asked the students to give me a brief account of what had happened in town, and told them that I would deal with them on Monday after I had a chance to talk to the Parkston police as well as their bus chaperone.

During this delay, one of the boys insisted that he be let off the bus.

I did not consent, and he became physically and verbally abusive. The situation escalated rapidly, and within the moment he was hands and knees on a bus seat trying to bash his head through a side glass window.

I quickly tried to restrain him by wrapping my arms around him and at the same time asked the chaperone to dismiss the remaining students. I also asked the driver to call for the BIA (Bureau of Indian Affairs) police. Minutes later the police arrived and took the boy with them.

Around 1:00 a.m. that morning the phone rang. The caller said that she was the boy's aunt, and that when she was through with me, I wouldn't have a shirt left on my back. The phone rang again about an hour later. It was the *Sioux Falls Argus Leader*. The conversation went like this as best I can recall.

"Is this Roger Wiltz, the Wagner school principal?" asked the caller.

"Yes it is," I replied.

"Were you involved in an incident on a school bus last night?"

"Yes I was. Let me tell you about it," I responded.

"We have our story." The caller hung up.

According to the *Argus Leader* headlines the next two days, the Wagner school principal had physically beaten a Native American youth.

The following Monday night there was a special school board meeting in the packed school theatre. The school's attorneys instructed me to say nothing about the incident to anyone. That was difficult as I wanted to defend myself. Yankton Sioux tribal leadership asked for a full investigation, and the school board granted their request.

During the week our home's sliding glass door was bashed in. I received countless death threats on the phone. Sitting in my office while the investigation took place down the hall was a week from hell. I was told nothing.

The students I retained on the bus would be key witnesses. They would be under intense pressure. Could they truthfully relate what happened on that dark bus?

During an afternoon late that week school board president Dave Robertson came into my office. I had been found innocent of all charges. In fact, my handling of the incident was praised considering the time I had to make decisions. On the following Tuesday, a postage stamp-sized notice on a back page in *The Argus Leader* cleared my name.

The bruises on the boy's head were self-inflicted by the bus window, not from me. Thank-you Indian Health Services! The students disclosed that the boy had drunk a bottle of Ever Clear, a 200 proof alcohol product.

The story was far-reaching. Supt. Hall learned of it on television while elk hunting in Colorado. Former friends and acquaintances learned of my whereabouts and sent letters of support.

It is my hope that as a result of this story, the media might take a longer look at stories, especially when a person's reputation is at stake, before jumping to conclusions.

Life Isn't Fair

If I could go back and relive any of my past fishing adventures, it wouldn't be the Amazon or Zambesi Rivers, the Queen Charlotte Islands, or Reindeer Lake. No, I'd be a kid sitting on the dock at Cedar Lake, Indiana. Janet, my little sister, would be seated next to me, and I'd be baiting her bamboo pole or removing a perch from her hook.

While I was fishing with friends on Sunday afternoon, May 20th, my sister, Janet, passed away. In a manner of speaking, I've been "fishing" all my life while my sister spent much of her time suffering.

Back in 1955, when I was an eighth grader, our mother began to notice some troubling symptoms. Numbness was developing in her legs, and a car accident followed when she missed the brake pedal. Dad took her to the best hospitals, including the Mayo Clinic, in an effort to get a diagnosis. Eventually we learned that mom had multiple sclerosis. Her deterioration was rapid.

When I left home for college in Brookings, SD in 1960, mom was using a walker. Within a year she was wheelchair bound. As an eleven-year-old, Janet, my sister, was doing much of the laundry and housekeeping, helping with supper, and assisting with our four-year-old baby brother. Dad took over when he got home from work at night, but Janet still had as much responsibility as any adult.

Janet's high school years began in 1962. She arranged her schedule so she could come home at noon and take over the household chores as well as care for mom. There was no time for school activities in her life.

I didn't get home from Brookings very often, and for the most part, I dodged the burden that had fallen on the rest of the family. However, I have never forgotten what Janet told me during one of my infrequent visits. She looked me in the eye and said, "I hope you have some idea of how lucky you are to walk out of this place and go back to South Dakota." Mom mercifully died in 1966. I'm thankful she had the chance to see her first grandchild.

Twenty-two years ago Janet was diagnosed with multiple sclerosis. Like my mom's illness, her condition deteriorated rapidly, and she spent much of her time confined to a wheelchair and then a bed. Over the years Jan's toughness and attitude have amazed, if not inspired me. I'm thankful for her second husband, Bill – a role model for the words, "for better or worse, in sickness and in health."

My sister loved fishing, and for a short period in her life her family had a cabin on southern Wisconsin's Rock River where she eagerly awaited the spring run of white bass. Maybe that's why the white bass is one of my favorite fish.

Janet taught me that life isn't fair – something I tried to teach my students over the years. The next time I think that I've been dealt a bad hand, I'll remember my sister. I hope you do too.

John Wiltz with 7 of his 9 grandchildren. Front: Lisa Wiltz, Jonny Adams, Julie Adams. Middle: Dana Wiltz, LuAnn Wiltz. Back: Leslie Wiltz, Grandpa, Laurie Wiltz

The Yankton Sioux Tribe

To live in Wagner for 42 years is to be affected by the presence of The Yankton Sioux Tribe. The headquarters for the Yankton Sioux Tribe are located just south of Wagner, SD. While traces of The Yankton Sioux Reservation still exist as there are pieces of Indian land within the original boundaries, it is my perception that The Yankton Sioux Reservation was slowly dissolved when reservation lands were sold to settlers.

My so-called "dissolving" of the original 1858 boundaries of The Yankton Sioux Reservation began with the Dawes Act of 1887.

"Pressure from westward bound homesteaders, and the belief that the Indians would benefit from private property ownership, promoted passage of The Dawes Act. The Dawes Act permitted the Federal Government to allot tracts of tribal land (160 acres) to individual Indians and, with tribal consent, to open the remaining holdings to non-Indian settlement."….. "In accordance with the Dawes Act, each member of the Yankton Tribe received a 160 acre tract from the existing reservation….. Members of the tribe acquired parcels of land throughout the 1858 reservation, although many of the allotments were clustered in the southern part near the Missouri River. By 1890, the allotting agent had apportioned 167,325 acres of reservation land. 95,000 additional acres were subsequently allotted under the Act of February 28, 1891…..and a small acreage was reserved for government and religious purposes. The surplus amounted to approximately 168,000 acres of unallotted lands."

Article II of the Dawes Act states: In consideration of the lands ceded, sold, relinquished, and conveyed to the United States, the U.S. agrees to pay the Yankton tribe $600,000.

Article VII states: In addition to the stipulations in the preceding articles, the U.S. will pay as follows: To each person whose name is signed to this agreement and to each other male member of the tribe who is 18 years old or older at the date of this agreement, twenty dollars ($20) in one double eagle, struck in the year 1892 as a memorial of this agreement.

Those $20 gold pieces must have "burned a hole" in many pockets. Today I wonder how many of those original double eagles still exist locally. I'd like to see one.

When we purchased different properties in Wagner, we noted that an Indian name often appeared in the origin of the abstract. I often wondered why an Indian had original ownership until reading the Dawes Act.

I don't know if the more or less recent Supreme Court ruling further weakened the concept of a Yankton Sioux Reservation, but this is how it went.

The Supreme Court of the United States began hearing the case SOUTH DAKOTA v. THE YANKTON SIOUX TRIBE on December 8, 1997. Their decision was rendered on January 26, 1998.

In this case, tribal, federal, and state officials disagreed as to the environmental regulations applicable to a solid waste disposal facility that lies on unallotted, non-Indian fee land, but falls within the reservation's original 1858 boundaries. This facility lies just west of Lake Andes, SD. The Tribe and the Federal Government contended that the site remains part of the reservation and is therefore subject to federal environmental regulations. The State maintained that the 1894 divestiture of Indian property diminished the Tribe's territory, and that the ceded lands no longer constitute "Indian Country."

In writing the Supreme Court's decision, Justice O'Connor made an interesting note. She wrote that back then, some members of Congress speculated that "Close contact with the frugal, moral, and industrious people who will settle on the reservation would stimulate individual effort and make the Tribe's progress much more rapid than heretofore." Did that happen? To a degree I suppose it did.

The Supreme Court ruled for the STATE OF SOUTH DAKOTA, a decision that would trickle down and affect other jurisdictional issues.

I don't claim that 42 years in Wagner have made me an authority on Indian affairs, but I do know that my 21 years as a school principal put me in close contact with Native American children, their families, their homes, their joys, and their sorrows on a daily basis.

It was enough time to realize that our federal government's handling of Indian affairs is an on-going miserable failure. While I expect Yankton Sioux tribal members to take offense to my calling the government's handling of Indian affairs a miserable failure, I want them to think about this.

Conservatively, I would estimate that the life expectancy of a Yankton Sioux tribal member is half that of the national average..... less than forty years! And that's with the readily available health care facilities! If I am anywhere near correct, how does one defend the current system?

James A. Michener, author of *Centennial,* summed up the solution to the problem quite well in the final passages of his classic on America when he said,

"And even though we signed the land treaties with the best intentions in the world, the wisest of the white men, at the very moment of the signing, knew that the papers weren't worth a damn. Before the ink was dry, the Indian was dispossessed."

"At last I know what I think about the American Indian. Every reservation in the nation should be closed down. The land should be distributed to the Indians, and if some of them wish to continue living communally, they should be encouraged, like the Pueblos in New Mexico. The rest should enter the dominant culture, to sink or swim as their talents determine. The way my family had to."

"Many good things will be lost, but the best will persist – in legend, in remembered ways of doing things, in our attitude toward the land. I can no longer support a system which keeps Indians apart, like freaks of nature. They aren't whooping cranes, to be preserved until the last one dies out. They're part of the mainstream, and that's where they belong."

Michener refers to the Indian people as "freaks of nature." Is this the common but despicable perception? It probably is. As a youth, I couldn't wait to visit my grandmother in Oklahoma City as I wanted to see a real Indian. When she pointed out a man on a downtown street as an Indian, I was disappointed. He looked like a typical person. No war bonnet, no paint. It wasn't until I was a freshman at South Dakota State that I further realized that Indians were ordinary people. I owe this enlightenment to my friends George Boltz from Igloo and Mike Ryan from Mobridge.

A look at the Treaty of 1859 tells us about the establishment of the Yankton Sioux Reservation and the Yankton Sioux Tribe. In late 1857, Chief Struck by the Ree went to Washington to negotiate a treaty. When he returned home, he told his people, "The white men are coming in like maggots. It is useless to resist them. They are many more than we are."

As the government wanted to open Indian lands that amounted to much of Eastern South Dakota (11.5 million acres) for expansion, they offered "Old Strike" as he was called, a 475,000 acre reservation in what would become Charles Mix County. Along with the acreage came a $1.6 million dollar payment in the form of a 50 year annuity. There was also the promise of education and health care. The Sioux moved onto their new reservation on July 10, 1859. Charles Mix represented the U.S. Government at the treaty signing. This promise of education and health care no doubt led to the facilities we see in Wagner today.

In my estimation, Struck by the Ree is the key figure in Yankton Sioux history. When Lewis and Clark stopped at the mouth of the James River in August 1804 to meet with the Sioux, they learned that a baby had just been born. They called for the baby, wrapped him in an American flag, and proclaimed him an American citizen. That baby was Struck by the Ree.

Other than being instrumental in the formation of the Yankton reservation, Struck or "Old Strike" was somewhat responsible for the ancestry of today's families that settled in the area.

At the beginning of the Minnesota Sioux outbreak and massacre of 1862, runners were sent to the Yanktons to ask that they take part in the killing raids. These raids were to include the settlements of Yankton, Vermillion, Bon Homme, and the settlers along the Big Sioux and James Rivers. As chief, Struck by the Ree called for a council. He persuaded the council not to join their Santee brothers in the raiding, and sent the runners home with that message. Struck, who changed the course of our history, is buried at Greenwood.

Michener mentioned that the best of tradition will persist should our federal government's abominable system of Indian management be shut down. I've become aware of bits and pieces of tradition.

Extended Family is a basic of Yankton Sioux family structure. Cousins are accepted as brothers and sisters. Aunts, and often grandmothers, are often unofficial heads of families. There is an apparent lacking presence of male or fatherly support. This made my dealing with truancy a difficult task as pinning down legal guardians was a challenging problem.

A tradition that I have admired over the years is called a Give Away. Pat Whitehorse, a school co-worker and personal friend, lost her two sons, Larry and Calvin Picotte, in a tragic automobile accident. At the first year anniversary of the accident, Pat hosted a Give Away at the Ft. Randall campground. Betsy and I were invited guests. Other than the serving of traditional food, Pat presented gifts to individual guests. It was her way of thanking all those who supported her during her loss. The gift was also significant in that when the gift was used, it would bring back the memory of the boys. It did exactly that! When we use that blue woolen blanket, we think of those boys.

I also became acquainted with the Feather Ceremony. This ritual involved the presentation of an eagle feather to the one being honored for a significant accomplishment. That accomplishment was most often high school graduation, and I realized that being invited to a Feather Ceremony was an honor reserved for those most highly respected by the recipient.

When I agree with Michener that the federal government's reservation system must be closed down, I'm basing that opinion on what I have personally seen.

The system is a fertile breeding grounds for neglect abuse, child abuse, sexual abuse, spousal abuse, alcohol abuse, and substance abuse, not to mention the squandering and misappropriation of millions and millions of dollars. It strips individuals of dignity, pride, and self-worth. I could relate a number of gut-wrenching stories, but they would serve no purpose. This travesty has nothing to do with race. I believe that any culture forced into this environment would suffer the same fate.

The dual system of law enforcement, with jurisdiction being a constant problem, is a travesty. Meth is a major problem, and seeing a joint force come down and crush the illicit manufacturers and distributors just isn't happening.

On the plus side, over my past 42 years in Wagner I have observed some forward progress with regard to the Yankton Sioux. Housing is a significant element.

Greenwood is a beautiful area south by southwest of Wagner that lies along the original banks of the Missouri River. In 1969-1970, twenty-five two, three, and four bedroom homes were built in Greenwood. The homes, owned by the Yankton Sioux Housing Authority, had full basements with yards, concrete streets, and curb and gutter. Other tribal buildings included a law enforcement facility, a commodities distribution center that never opened because of constant break-ins, and a beautiful tribal hall of contemporary tee-pee design. When we came to Wagner in the summer of 1976, the majority of the homes/buildings in the multi-million dollar Greenwood project had already been destroyed.

It appears to me that tribal leadership is slowly learning that buildings and grounds tend to fare better when residents have a stake in the ownership. Today the number of Wagner homes owned by tribal members has increased, and the general appearance of these homes is commendable.

From the very beginning of my tenure as high school principal, I learned to hate what the YST called "claims money." What it amounted to was this: On his/her 18th birthday, a Yankton Sioux member was given a very substantial sum of money. In most cases, it led a successful senior student to drop out of school. In many instances, it led directly to their deaths.

A few people, myself included, attempted to solve the problem by getting the YST to set high school graduation or 21 years of age as the claims money standard. The measure was brought to the YST membership for a vote, and it failed to pass. Today the claims money check is a thing of the past – a substantial improvement in tribal affairs.

In all things, education is the key to an improved life style. So it is for the Yankton Sioux students in the Wagner Community School. In looking at a 1978 Wagner High School annual, only 10% of the high school students were Native American. Today it is 66%.

These students are participating in extra-curricular activities, posting excellent achievement test scores, graduating, and successfully moving on to post-secondary institutions. We will steadily observe the positive fruits of their labor. The YST's future lies in their hands, and I feel good about it. I'm very proud of the fact, that according to Sebastian Junger, author of *Tribe*, American Indians, proportionately, provide more soldiers to America's wars than any other demographic group in our country. This is evident in our Wagner school.

The problems I have alluded to are all of our faults. Other than signed treaties, most of which were never honored in the first place, I don't understand why our people in Congress, particularly our two senators, don't form a lobby with other reservations states and demand change. You and I are at fault for enabling the current debacle to persist.

Tripp-Delmont School — Golden Years in Education

When I retired as the Wagner high school principal in the spring of 1997, I was 55 years old and eligible for full retirement benefits. My retirement was not an easy decision as the school board had offered me my best raise in my 21 years. Equally significant, the board offered to accept my resignation, re-hire me, and enable me to collect retirement benefits as well as my salary. After much deliberation, I chose retirement. My decision was made easier by the fact that Neil Goter, the very capable assistant principal, would take over. The school was my "baby," and leaving it was not easy. Neil made it easier.

Though I had fishing, golf, hunting, and some travel in mind, Betsy often reminded me that I had some good years left in me and that I could still help some young people. With these thoughts in mind, I kept my eyes open to new opportunity.

Midway through the summer I learned that the Tripp-Delmont School, 26 miles away, had an opening for High School English/ Guidance Counselor. I was certified in Guidance and I was an English major with a SD Lifetime Teacher's Certificate. I met with T-D superintendent Glen Schneider, and we talked about the position.

The thought of the 26 mile drive didn't bother me. In fact, I saw it as a chance to plan my day in detail. Truth be told, a number of pheasants and some spring snow geese fell victim to that cross country return trip home.

On my first day in the classroom, I had written a significant sum of money on the chalkboard in big letters. When asked what that was all about. I told them,

"That's the amount of the retirement check I receive in the mail every month. I don't need this job. If I get fired, I'll go home and sleep well. Don't ever get smart-mouthed with me, and don't ever lie to me." It was the beginning of a six-year mutual admiration relationship.

Switching to a lower paying job hurt my retirement check as retirement pay was based on the highest paying years. It didn't take me long to realize that personal satisfaction was far more important than money.

I soon learned that Tripp-Delmont was a great school with many veteran teachers. I pushed myself to meet their standards and competency. T-D had a great high school band under Wayne Dempster's leadership. Most every one of my junior-high career class students told me that band was the coolest thing at T-D High. My short T-D tenure included a number of state football championships, a boys basketball championship, and a girls basketball trip to state. I also spent two years as T-D's junior high football coach. I obviously have fond memories of those years.

Thanks to teachers like Ray Hanson, T-D High was an academic gold mine. ACT scores were typically in the high 20's with 30 or above occurring quite often. I was a small part of that as I coached the juniors in taking that test.

T-D High gave me the opportunity to try in the classroom what I had been thinking about after 26 years of evaluating teachers. I learned that kids like to work hard, and I learned that the students will achieve what you expect of them.

Like my Parkston students, my English class students received a syllabus on Monday morning that included the twenty vocabulary words they were to define, spell, and use in a sentence. The syllabus also included the essay topic for the week, a topic I felt was relevant and thought-provoking. Essays were collected on Friday morning and returned on Monday with corrections and recommendations. We also read novels I felt were significant.

Other than my chosen novels and vocabulary-essay assignments, we adhered to the state requirement/curriculum demands. My students happily did twice the work most students did. I found it interesting that some of the moms wanted to write about my essay topics and have me look over their papers. I appreciated their interest and support, but enough was enough!

It is my hope that my T-D students can look back at those years with the same positive feelings I shared with you today.

Rotary

Though I became a Wagner Rotarian in the early '80's, I wasn't very active until retirement other than being a district exchange student co-chair. Our three daughters did make year-long exchanges that positively affected their lives. Laurie went to Colombia, Lisa to Mexico, and LuAnn to Argentina. They learned to speak Spanish fluently.

In 2006-2007, I was Governor of District 5610 – a district that included all of South Dakota, and parts of Western Minnesota, Northern Iowa, and a portion of Nebraska. Today I try to remain as active as possible as I believe that The Rotary Foundation is the most efficient foundation in the world.

Epilogue

Today Betsy and I continue to reside in Wagner, SD where I enjoy golf, fishing, and hunting with friends. I also strive to improve my writing as I continue with my weekly outdoor column.

We have a second home in Mt. Horeb, WI that enables us to spend more time with daughters Lisa and LuAnn and their families. Proximity to the U. of Wisconsin Hospital has been a godsend as I had a serious bout with melanoma skin cancer as well as Deep Brain Stimulation surgery to deal with my Essential Tremor.

Our three daughters are graduates of the University of South Dakota. Laurie Fisher, our oldest, is a family practice physician in the Kansas City area whose excellence has been recognized by her peers. Dr. Laurie also delivers babies. Laurie and her husband, Jamie, have two daughters, Hannah and Madison.

Lisa Ladson, our middle daughter, is a behavior analyst dealing specifically with autism. Her co-authored book, *Lights, Camera, Autism,* has been very successful. During the summer of 2018, Lisa lost her husband, Rodney, to heart failure. Chef Rod was one of the most liked people I have ever known. Rod and Lisa have one daughter, Nichela.

LuAnn Shay, our youngest daughter, was a Certified Physician's Assistant who spent 20 years in family practice and reconstructive surgery before pursuing a new career in investment counseling. Tom, her ex, and Lu have three children including Sam, the oldest, and identical twins Grace and Gabrielle. During the 2017-2018 Christmas break, Lu married Dr. Mark Markel, Dean of the UW Veterinary School. It would be difficult to not like everything about Mark.

Lightning Source UK Ltd.
Milton Keynes UK
UKHW040603270219
338085UK00003B/63/P

9 781546 277675